THE GREAT TEA PARTY
IN THE OLD NORTHWEST

To Bob
Best wishes.

THE GREAT TEA PARTY
IN THE OLD NORTHWEST

STATE CONSTITUTIONAL CONVENTIONS, 1847–1851

David M. Gold

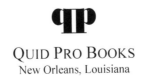

QUID PRO BOOKS
New Orleans, Louisiana

Published in 2015 by Quid Pro Books.

ISBN 978-1-61027-294-0 (pbk.)
ISBN 978-1-61027-295-7 (ebk.)

QUID PRO BOOKS
5860 Citrus Blvd.
Suite D-101
New Orleans, Louisiana 70123
www.quidprobooks.com

Publisher's Cataloging in Publication

Gold, David M., 1950-
    The Great Tea Party in the Old Northwest : State Consti-
    tutional Conventions, 1847-1851 / David M. Gold.

        p. cm. — (History & heroes)

    Includes bibliographical references.

    ISBN 978-1-61027-294-0 (pbk.)

1. Northwest, Old—History. 2. United States—Northwest, Old.
3. Constitutional conventions—U.S. states. I. Title. II.
Series.

F479 H4 .G65 2015   2015377289

Cover artwork, "A watercolor view of Madison [Wisc.] by Johann B. Wengler, an Austrian who traveled in America, 1850–1851," showing the second Capitol (where the convention was held 1846–1847) and its Madison environs on King Street, is housed by the Oberoesterreichisches Landesmuseum, Linz, Austria.

Map images are used by permission of Barry Lawrence Ruderman Antique Maps, *www.RareMaps.com*. Author photograph in back cover inset reprinted courtesy of Kristin Rhee. Other images are reprinted from public domain sources.

Portions of the author's work have been republished in modified form in chapters 2, 3, and 8 and are used by permission of the previous publishers: *Democracy in Session: A History of the Ohio General Assembly* (copyright © 2009, Ohio University Press, *www.ohioswallow.com*), and "Eminent Domain and Economic Development: The Mill Acts and the Origins of Laissez-Faire Constitutionalism," *Journal of Libertarian Studies* 21 (Summer 2007): 101-122 (a publication of the Mises Institute).

CONTENTS

Author's Note

I work for a nonpartisan state legislative agency. My coworkers and I are very scrupulous about avoiding political activity other than voting. We do not attend political rallies, put bumper stickers on our cars, or sign petitions. I am confident that the politicians for whom we work have no idea of our political affiliations. To the best of my recollection, I have never publicly endorsed or condemned the Tea Party, and this book is not intended to help or hinder the Tea Party cause. It is a work of popular history, not polemics.

I have long been interested in nineteenth-century state constitutional conventions. My first published writing on the subject appeared in 1985, long before the modern Tea Party arose. As the Tea Party came to prominence in recent years, I was struck by the similarity of the issues that roused critics of state government in the mid-nineteenth century and those that motivate the Tea Partiers of today. The nineteenth-century "Tea Party" movement helped bring about a spate of state constitutional conventions that shaped the constitutions of new states and dramatically rewrote the fundamental laws of many older ones. Those conventions are unknown to most Americans today. In view of the modern Tea Party's continuing impact on politics—I write this just days after little-known David Brat, with Tea Party support, defeated the majority leader of the U.S. House of Representatives in a primary—the time seemed right to bring the historical precedent to light.

When I refer to the nineteenth-century drive for constitutional conventions as a Tea Party movement and to the constitutions adopted as Tea Party constitutions, I do not mean to suggest that there was such a phenomenon as a Tea Party, in the current sense of the term, 165 years ago. The Tea Party is a product of advanced technology: cable television, cell phones, and the Internet. Furthermore, its grass roots can be measured by sophisticated public opinion polls, which did not exist in 1850. But the proponents of constitutional reform in the mid-nineteenth century rode a wave of popular anger toward government not so different from the hostility displayed by Tea Partiers today. The grounds for that antagonism were similar in important ways to those underlying the Tea Party's disgust with government, and some of the most important constitutional changes they wrought resembled the reforms demanded by the Tea Party today. Hence my use of the anachronistic "Tea Party" as a tag for the convention movement.

In an effort to keep this book short and simple, I have kept the documentation to a minimum. The few endnotes are to document direct quotations or specific facts derived from modern sources. Most of the older, undocumented quotes can be readily tracked down by a web search. The bibliographical note at the end of the book will guide readers to the major sources used.

D.M.G.

THE GREAT TEA PARTY
IN THE OLD NORTHWEST

1

Introduction

A sympathetic commentator on the modern Tea Party movement, law professor Elizabeth Price Foley, observes in *The Tea Party: Three Principles* that the movement has three core tenets: limited government, U.S. sovereignty, and a constitutional interpretation based on the Constitution's original meaning. And of these, the dominant theme is limited government. Indeed, the second and third principles are really variants of the first. The aim of globalists, writes Foley, is to "bulk up" government through the idea of global sovereignty. The theory of a "living Constitution," which rejects originalism in favor of a flexible, evolving interpretation, allows judges to disregard the limits on government that the drafters built into the Constitution.

For all her insistence on America's limited-government tradition, Foley actually understates the scope of that heritage. The idea of limited government, according to Foley, stems from the Constitution's "unique concept of a government"—a *federal* government—"that possesses only limited and enumerated powers." As for the states, Foley writes that the principle of limited government doesn't apply to them. Similarly, Tea Party activist Michael Patrick Leahy, in *Covenant of Liberty: The Ideological Origins of the Tea Party Movement*, excoriates politicians from Alexander Hamilton to Barack Obama for violating key constitutional principles, but he focuses exclusively on the actions of national leaders and the federal government. He has nothing to say about state politics, state constitutions, or protests at the state level.

Nor, more surprisingly, do historians Jill Lepore and Ronald P. Formisano. Lepore, a professor of history at Harvard University, criticizes the Tea Party's "historical fundamentalism" in *The Whites of Their Eyes: The Tea Party's Revolution and the Battle over American History*. Everyone knows that Tea Partiers

1

venerate "the founding." After all, their movement is named for the famous Boston event of 1773 that set the colonies on the road to revolution. Lepore quotes a modern-day Tea Partier who, having recently read a biography of Samuel Adams, pronounced, "It's the same exact issues, all over again." Yet Lepore herself says little about the more than two and a quarter centuries that elapsed between the Boston Tea Party and the publication of her book. Formisano, of the University of Kentucky, is a respected historian who has written about populist movements in America in the first half of the nineteenth century, but he barely mentions them in his history of the Tea Party. Historians Elliot A. Rosen and Charles Postel locate the origins of the Tea Party movement in the 1930s, when, according to Rosen, Republicans committed themselves to limiting "federal intrusion into the rights of the states, corporations, and the individual." Could these omissions by Lepore, Formisano, Rosen, and Postel be based on the fact that nineteenth-century versions of the Tea Party movement were aimed at the state governments rather than the federal government?

Although some New Yorkers who were angry at their state government held a Tea Party protest in January 2009, a month before the event that sparked the nationwide Tea Party movement, it is true that the modern Tea Party aims most of its ire at the federal government. After all, it is the federal government, with its huge bureaucracy and enormous power, its stimulus plans and far-reaching regulations, that imposes most heavily on citizens today. But Americans have been protesting against the heavy hand of government since long before the federal government became a behemoth. Suppose someone approached you today and announced, "We have to take away from government as much temptation to the abuse of power as possible. We should leave corporations to get along on their own, without any help from government. Debt contracting and money squandering have to be ended for good. The whole system must be dug up by the roots, and no single sprout ever permitted to shoot up again." You might think that you were confronting a Tea Partier of the first order, angry over the Obama administration's bailouts of banks and insurance companies during the financial crisis of 2008–09, the huge national debt, and the scandal of Solyndra, a well-connected company that went bankrupt after receiving hundreds of millions of dollars in federal aid. In fact, these words come, only slightly modified, from the published debates of the Ohio constitutional convention of 1850–51.

The Ohio gathering was one of many state constitutional conventions held in the middle of the nineteenth century. Not even counting the conventions called to draft constitutions for new states, we find such assemblies held in New Jersey in 1844, Missouri in 1845, New York in 1846, Illinois in 1847, and Kentucky in 1849. In 1850 alone, conventions met in Indiana, Maryland, Michigan, New Hampshire, Ohio, Vermont, and Virginia. Most of them had as major themes the need to limit government and to make public officials more accountable to the people. The agitation for constitutional reform, culminating in all those conventions, was the Tea Party movement of the nineteenth century.

Tea Partiers love history and often resort to the ideas and documents of the Founders. Foley defends this reliance on our eighteenth-century forebears, while Lepore criticizes it as anti-historical. Any Tea Partier who reads Lepore's critique should find it disturbing. According to Lepore, the Tea Party's view of the past fails to account for changes in context. It suffers from "historical fundamentalism," a belief that "the founding" is "ageless and sacred," that the Founding Fathers were divinely inspired, and that certain founding documents must be read in the same spirit with which religious fundamentalists read scripture. Evidence that the Revolutionary era may have been less than ideal or that the Founders had nothing to say about current issues does not interest Tea Party types, Lepore claims. They ignore such inconvenient facts as the legally inferior position of women and the existence of slavery, even in Massachusetts, in the 1770s. They confidently assert, as conservative commentator Glenn Beck did, that George Washington would have opposed socialism. In fact, writes Lepore, it is impossible to know what any eighteenth-century American would have thought of twenty-first-century stimulus plans, wars, or concealed-carry laws.

There is good reason for the Tea Party's frequent allusions to the Revolutionary generation and to the nation's founding principles. The Founders were intelligent men who had no illusions about their ability to predict the future. They knew that time would require flexibility in the application of their political principles. But they also believed that their ideals of liberty and republican government were indeed "ageless and sacred." The Virginia Declaration of Rights of 1776 admonished that the preservation of free government and the blessings of liberty required "a frequent recurrence to fundamental principles." Other early state constitutions included similar language, as did the constitutions of several states that joined the Union in the nineteenth and twentieth centuries. People may disagree over the meaning of those fundamental principles or their application to modern circumstances, but to disregard the foundational principles of American government is to invite an anything-goes approach to government. It is hardly a sin for Tea Partiers to revere the principles of the founding and to try to maintain them in the face of perceived threats to their continued viability.

Besides, America's fundamental principles have stood the country in good stead. Bringing the no-taxation-without-representation argument to the cause of woman suffrage, Susan B. Anthony asked, "What was the three-penny tax on tea, or the paltry tax on paper and sugar to which our Revolutionary fathers were subjected, when compared with the taxation of the women of this republic?" And what was at the heart of the twentieth-century civil rights movement, if not the tenet of the Declaration of Independence that all men are created equal?

But justifying a recurrence to America's founding principles is hardly a sufficient response to Lepore's critique. U.S. Supreme Court justice Owen Roberts once famously wrote that when a court was confronted with a challenge to the constitutionality of a statute, the court had but one duty: "to lay the article of the Constitution which is invoked beside the statute which is challenged and to decide whether the latter squares with the former." The statement has often been criticized for ignoring the vagueness of many constitutional provisions and the accumulation of gloss

4

over the many generations since the Constitution was written. By the same token, America's "fundamental principles," whether or not expressly enshrined in a constitution, acquire meaning over time. Or perhaps their meaning is validated and reinforced.

The appropriate response to Lepore's critique is to examine the history of those principles in action. Is there in fact a tradition of Tea Party movements, impelled by causes and animated by ideas similar to those that created the twenty-first-century Tea Party? Is there something in the long interval between 1773 and 2009 that links the Tea Party movement to the founding? Or is the Tea Party's recitation of fundamental principles ritualistic and ahistorical? A partial answer lies in the state constitutional conventions of the mid-nineteenth century. They are precedents for today's Tea Party movement, ones that are more relevant than the Boston Tea Party for which the movement is named. The purpose of this book is neither to endorse nor to denigrate the constitutional conventions or the Tea Party. It is simply to highlight a part of American history that bears on one of the most important political phenomena of our time—to show that today's Tea Party is not the first one we've had since 1773.

On December 16, 1773, American colonists disguised as Indians clambered aboard three British merchant ships and emptied the contents of 342 chests of tea into Massachusetts Bay to ensure that the tax on the tea would not be paid. The incident became the most famous tax protest in American history, but it wasn't really a demonstration against the financial burden of the tax, which was quite small. The real issue was taxation without representation.

The Boston Tea Party arose out of an attempt by the British Parliament to bail out the financially distressed East India Company. The company had a monopoly on British trade with Asia. By the 1760s England had become a nation of tea-drinkers. The American colonies had adopted the habit as well. But tea was heavily taxed, and smugglers made enormous profits selling tea in both the mother country and the colonies. Smuggling deprived the East India Company of sales and the British government of tax revenue. Prohibited by law from shipping tea directly to America, the company auctioned its tea to London merchants, who in turn sold the tea to merchants in the colonies, mostly in Boston, New York, and Philadelphia. But because smuggled tea dominated the colonial market, the company's warehouses in London bulged with an unsalable product.

Smuggling was an old problem in America and had already led to constitutional conflicts. In 1733 Parliament levied a heavy duty on molasses and sugar imported into the British colonies from the French and Spanish West Indies. American distillers used molasses to make rum, a business made highly profitable by the use of smuggled and therefore untaxed molasses. In 1760 customs officials searching for smuggled molasses employed writs of assistance, general search warrants that allowed them to search any place at any time. Boston lawyer James Otis argued valiantly in court that writs of assistance violated both English and natural law. He lost the case, but his fiery arguments reinforced Americans' hatred of the writs.

In need of revenue, Parliament lowered the duties on sugar and molasses in 1764, but it levied a host of new taxes on imported goods and placed new restrictions on exports from the colonies. The Sugar Act also created vice-admiralty courts to try violators. These courts functioned without juries. The Act prompted a movement to boycott the taxed products. Parliament eventually lowered the molasses duty again, but not until after Americans rose up in protest against the Stamp Act. Unlike the sugar and molasses duties, which were regulations of commerce, the Stamp Act taxed Americans directly by requiring that revenue stamps be purchased and placed on all kinds of paper items, from newspapers to legal documents to playing cards. The Stamp Act provoked boycotts more effective than those against the Sugar Act. It also induced riots and threats of violence against the stamp commissioners, and it united efforts by the colonies.

The Stamp Act raised new constitutional issues. Because it was an "internal" tax imposed directly on the colonists in America and not on imports, it could not be construed as a trade regulation. It was, argued opponents of the Act, a tax levied on Americans without their consent. Consent could be given through elected representatives, but the colonists did not send representatives to

Parliament. Prime Minister George Grenville insisted that Americans enjoyed "virtual representation" because all members of Parliament represented all Englishmen. Long used to governing themselves through their elected colonial assemblies, Americans had little use for the theory of virtual representation. They resented the imposition of burdens by members of Parliament who lived three thousand miles across the ocean and knew little of America and American conditions. To the colonists, taxation by "virtual" representatives was not taxation with the consent of the taxed.

The resistance to the Stamp Act led Parliament to repeal the measure, but in 1767 Parliament tried again with the Townshend Acts. These laws levied duties on a variety of products imported by the colonies, including a small tax on tea. As "external" taxes, the British thought, the duties should not raise serious objections. One of the stated purposes of the Townshend duties was to provide a source of revenue for the support of governors and judges in America. This would make them independent of the colonial assemblies, which in most colonies paid the salaries of these officials. The ministry underestimated American opposition. Once again, raucous protests—and the economic interests of British merchants, who always suffered from the disruption of colonial trade—led to repeal. But Parliament insisted on leaving the tax on tea as a symbol of its right to tax the colonies. And British troops sent to Boston in 1768 to enforce the revenue laws remained in the city.

Relations between Great Britain and the colonies reached a low point in 1770 when a mob provoked soldiers into firing into the crowd and killing five civilians. The episode became known as the Boston Massacre. The soldiers were tried for murder in a Massachusetts court. Most were acquitted following an able defense by James Otis and John Adams. The acquittals calmed nerves on both sides of the Atlantic. Despite continuing disturbances, including ongoing warfare between smugglers and customs officials and the burning of a British revenue cutter by colonists, the next three years were relatively quiet.

The troubles of the East India Company brought the tranquility to an end. The company needed a way to sell tea cheaply in

America—cheaply enough to undercut the smugglers. In May 1773 Parliament passed the Tea Act. The law lowered the price of East Indian tea by removing a duty on tea as it entered England from Asia and allowing the company to sell directly to American consumers instead of through middlemen. The Townshend tea tax remained in effect, but the British ministry believed that Americans would rather buy cheaper, better-quality tea legally than the inferior stuff sold by the smugglers—even if it meant paying a small tax.

Radicals in the colonies thought differently. The Tea Act gave them a means of reviving the fervor of the 1760s. When news of the Tea Act reached the colonies in the summer of 1773, the radicals whipped up all the old antagonisms. On October 16, a public meeting in Philadelphia adopted a series of resolutions laying out the case against the tea tax. The "disposal of their own property," read the resolutions, "is the inherent right of freemen." Parliament's taxation of Americans without their consent deprived the colonists of that inherent right. The tea tax would be used to support the British administration in the colonies—that is, to make royal officials independent of the colonial assemblies—and would "render assemblies useless" and "introduce arbitrary government and slavery." Americans had no choice but to oppose this "ministerial plan" if they were to "preserve even the shadow of liberty." Anyone who "directly or indirectly" countenanced or aided in the unloading or sale of the East India Company's tea while it remained subject to the tax was "an enemy to his country." On November 5, the selectmen of the Town of Boston adopted the Philadelphia Resolutions.

Bostonians demanded that the tea be sent back to Britain. However, there was a legal problem: the tea had to be unloaded and taxed within twenty days after arriving in port. After twenty days, revenue officers, backed by military force, would seize the cargo, take it to the customs house, and collect the tax. The night before the deadline, radical Bostonians had their Tea Party.

The tea tax alone would not have brought about the Boston Tea Party. As Thomas Jefferson would write in the Declaration of Independence, it takes "a long train of abuses" to overcome mankind's tendency "to suffer, while evils are sufferable." By late 1773, though, the "train of abuses" had grown long, indeed. In addition to the writs of assistance, revenue acts, and stationing of troops, there were restrictions on the westward migration of Americans, the suspension of the New York Assembly for failing to provide housing for British soldiers, and other irritants large and small. Americans had a penchant for violence that exasperated the British government, but patriots would lay the blame for the violence at the door of an officious, unrepresentative British government that repeatedly refused to address American petitions for relief. Sam Adams blamed the Boston Tea Party on "the consignees, together with the collector of the customs, and the governor of the province," who, by insisting that the tea be landed, "prevented the safe return of the East India Company's property . . . to London."

Beyond all the specific grievances that the colonists had, by the 1770s they harbored a deep distrust of British politicians. Many Americans felt sure that evil government ministers, a greedy "monied interest," a "junto of courtiers and state-jobbers" who had gotten the king's ear and gained control of Parliament "by power, interest, and application of the people's money to *placement* and *pensioners*," were out to destroy liberty and establish tyranny. The colonists who held such a jaundiced view of their British overlords could not be persuaded of the reasonableness of British revenue or law-enforcement measures in America. Nor would they believe that their own violent attempts to thwart the tyrannical ministers were unreasonable.

The British government reacted to the Boston Tea Party with a series of harsh measures known as the Coercive or Intolerable Acts. These laws closed the port of Boston, curtailed popular government in Massachusetts, and allowed the trial of royal officials accused of crimes to be held in other colonies or even in Great Britain. Together with other objectionable measures passed at the same time and a determination on the part of the ministry to finally bring the colonies to heel, the Intolerable Acts set the colonists on the road to revolution. Just ten months later, the Continental Congress declared economic war on Britain. A few months more brought the first shots of the Revolution at Lexington.

On December 16, 2007, the 234th anniversary of the Boston Tea Party, supporters of Congressman Ron Paul staged Tea Party reenactments in several cities. Paul himself appeared in Boston for the occasion. The events raked in more than $6 million in Internet contributions for his presidential campaign. On February 19, 2009, business reporter Rick Santelli, in an on-air "rant" on the floor of the Chicago Board of Trade, lambasted the Obama administration's handling of the mortgage crisis and called for a "Chicago Tea Party." In no time, Tea Party websites and Facebook groups sprang up. By April 15—tax day—more than 750 groups using Tea Party in their names had formed. The movement spawned an influential Tea Party Caucus in Congress and constant speculation, analysis, and punditry on the movement's impact on presidential elections. Yet for all its success, the movement remains classically populist, without central direction of any kind.

As a messy collection of like-minded groups lacking formal affiliation with one another, the movement has no official platform. Its major theme, though, is clear enough. The Tea Partiers want a smaller, less expensive, more accountable federal government. At a big Tea Party rally in Albany, New York, professional political observers Scott Rasmussen and Douglas Schoen heard the same complaints over and over again: "An unresponsive state and federal government. Policy makers simply ignoring their constituents. Taxpayers picking up the tab for costly legislative initiatives. The deck stacked against ordinary Americans." "Frankly I'm tired of being taxed," one protester explained. ". . . I want to see a lot less government in my life, period." Former congressman Dick Armey presents a similar litany: a stop to big government attacks on private property, less federal taxing and spending, more personal responsibility. "The Tea Party movement," says Armey, "is asking to simply be left alone."

Paul, Santelli, Armey, and the Tea Party movement generally take the Boston Tea Party as their inspiration. In 2010 a modern-day political organization calling itself the Boston Tea Party met to discuss the health-care bill then working its way through Congress.

A member who had recently read a biography of Samuel Adams remarked, "It's the same exact issues, all over again. They didn't like that the British government was trying to take over their lives." From 1773 to 2010—as if nothing had happened in between.

2

The Roots of the Convention Movement

In the middle of the nineteenth century, public disgust with government swept across the nation. Reflecting this revulsion, a delegate to one of those state constitutional conventions in 1850 demanded that the state legislature be stripped of much of its power. "We shall . . . take away from them as much as possible all temptation to the abuse of their powers," he exclaimed. "All this will be done with special reference to the complaints that we have too much legislation, which have come up from all quarters."

How did state governments—popularly elected governments, operating under constitutions drafted by elected convention delegates and in most cases ratified by the voters—come to be so reviled? And why did so many people want new constitutional conventions to remodel their governments? Scholars sometimes attribute the flurry of conventions in the 1840s and 1850s to Jacksonian Democracy, the political movement named for President Andrew Jackson, elected in 1828. The elements of Jacksonian Democracy were majority rule, the majority consisting of the "producing classes" of independent farmers and artisans; opposition to "associated wealth," especially in the form of banking corporations with special privileges; equal rights, at least for white men; states' rights; limited government; popular participation in government; territorial expansion; and a welcoming of white immigrants.[1]

Jacksonian Democracy certainly helped shape the convention movement, but general principles don't cause particular events. As Jefferson said, it takes a long train of specific abuses to make people act. The immediate causes of the conventions lay in a variety of citizens' complaints. Citizens moaned about nothing so much as the condition of state judicial systems, which could not keep up with the rapid growth in the nation's population, commerce, and the number of counties in which courts held sessions. A bill of grievances typical of the 1830s and 1840s, this one from Maine, lamented that cases generally took more than two years to conclude. The docket grew nonstop. Parties and witnesses had to travel from forty to sixty miles, wait weeks for their cases to come up, and often return home without getting a trial. "[A]nd if a person recovers," grumbled the disgruntled citizens, "his expenses exceed his claim in almost all cases, unless his demand is a large one, and when judgment is obtained the suit is only in its first stage; the expenses attached to it render the parties desperate, and appeal is generally made, and carried up to the Supreme Court, and our pockets are emptied by a privileged class [presumably, lawyers] at the expense of the laboring and business part of the community." Lawmakers often felt powerless to fix the problem because state constitutions limited their ability to modify judicial systems.

Some constitutional conventions resulted from longstanding gripes about legislative apportionment. As populations grew and shifted around, traditional methods of representation based on towns, parishes, or counties produced lopsided legislatures. In Virginia, the underrepresentation of western counties in the state legislature was a potent force in producing constitutional conventions in 1829–30 and again in 1850. In Rhode Island, malapportionment of the state legislature was one of two longstanding grievances—the other being restrictions on suffrage—that brought about the political and armed confrontation known as the Dorr Rebellion and finally, in 1842, constitutional reform.

It has been argued that the financial crisis known as the Panic of 1837 was the specific event that sparked the convention movement of the following decade. In this view, reckless state funding of "internal improvements," especially canals, roads, and railroads, led to enormous public debt. The Panic and the severe economic depression that followed after a short respite drove many states to default or to the edge of bankruptcy and caused huge increases in taxes. The people rose up in anger over public subsidization of economic development and demanded constitutional conventions to curtail legislative power.

Some constitutional conventions of the Jacksonian era (roughly 1828–50) were held for none of these reasons but as steps on the path toward statehood. Six U.S. territories and one independent country, Texas, held conventions between 1836 and 1849 to draft their first state constitutions. Iowa and Wisconsin held two conventions apiece because voters rejected the first constitutions they were offered.

The years 1844 to 1851 witnessed a slew of constitutional conventions in states and territories from Virginia to California and from New Hampshire to Louisiana, but the heart of constitution making lay in the Old Northwest. All five states carved out of the original Northwest Territory—Ohio, Indiana, Illinois, Michigan, and Wisconsin—held conventions and adopted new constitutions. Moreover, the contiguous states of Virginia (which bordered on Ohio before West Virginia seceded in 1863), Kentucky, and Missouri and the territory of Iowa also held conventions in those years.

The factors that led to the calling of constitutional conventions in the Old Northwest varied from place to place, as we will see in the discussions of the individual states. Having likened the convention movement to the modern Tea Party crusade, though, I want to focus on those issues that should most resonate with observers of today's Tea Party. They are first and foremost financial in nature: public debt, taxation, the proper role of government in economic matters, the relationship between government and corporations. It is true that some Tea Party groups include gun rights, traditional family values, immigration, and other social issues among their concerns, but there is no question that what really drives them is anger over the size and scope of government, especially with regard to taxing and spending. An early Tea Party activist, recalling the heady days of 2009, wrote three years later, "We labored mightily since the inception of the Nationwide Tea Party Coalition to make sure that everyone in the movement understood that we united around the fiscal issues. We would leave the social issues off the table until the fiscal and constitutional issues had been solved."[2] Besides, the main social issues of the Jacksonian era, liquor control and race, are only marginally relevant to today. Race is still important in the United States, of course, but the constitutional battles of the 1840s and 1850s mostly involved slavery, suffrage, and schools. Those battles ended long ago.

The nineteenth-century economic issues were all related to the schemes of "internal improvement"—the construction of a transportation network of turnpikes, canals, and railroads—that crashed almost everywhere. Nineteenth-century Americans also had complaints involving taxing and spending that were unconnected with internal improvements. For example, the traditional reliance on real property taxation grew steadily more unfair as the economy changed and wealth took forms other than land. But it was the internal improvements fiasco that fueled public ire against state legislatures.

Demands for greater accountability of government officials to the public accompanied the anger over the collapse of internal improvements. Traditionally, many public officials, such as judges, secretaries of state, and state treasurers, were appointed by the governor with the advice and consent of the state senate or were elected by state legislatures. A trend toward the popular election of more public officials set in years before the Panic of 1837, but it accelerated when constitutional conventions, triggered by other causes, seized the opportunity to reshape government in accordance with Jacksonian ideals. Changes in legislative procedure also flowed from the deep disgust with government. People wanted to ensure that legislative activity would be open and honest and that lawmakers would not legislate "by stealth."[3]

To understand the internal improvements controversy, we need to look more closely at the phenomenon of Jacksonian Democracy and to consider the history of government-sponsored economic development in America.

Jacksonian Democracy rested on the idea of equality. By Andrew Jackson's day, equality had become a cherished American ideal. Pulitzer Prize-winning historian Daniel Walker Howe refuses to use the term "Jacksonian Democracy" because of the deep racism and antifeminism harbored by most Democrats. However, even when limited to white males, equality was a mighty

American ideal. The "most radical and most powerful force let loose in the [American] Revolution . . . the idea of equality could not be stopped, and it tore through American society and culture with awesome power."[4] Politically, equality came to mean equal representation in government—a precursor to the twentieth-century concept of "one man, one vote"—and the right of all white men to vote, regardless of their economic status.

At the time of the Revolution, Americans rejected the British idea that all members of society were "virtually" represented by lawmakers they had had no say in electing. Virtual representation had led to the "rotten boroughs" of Britain, districts that had few residents but sent representatives to Parliament while some large cities sent no one. Americans demanded "actual representation"— representation by individuals who knew the interests of the electors and shared their concerns. Americans more and more thought of representation of people, not of property or geographical units such as boroughs. As egalitarian rhetoric and reform swept through America in the late eighteenth century, actual representation came to mean equal representation of people. Furthermore, although Americans often established property qualifications for voting and excluded various categories of people from the franchise, they increasingly demanded the abolition of such barriers.

Demands for universal white male suffrage drove some of the calls for conventions to revise existing state constitutions before 1840. In Connecticut, where the dominant Federalists had actually narrowed rather than expanded suffrage after the Revolution, the restricted franchise was an important factor in bringing about the constitutional convention of 1818. In Virginia, calls for broadened suffrage, backed by the old sage Thomas Jefferson, helped bring about the convention of 1829–30, which resulted in the reduction but not elimination of property qualifications for voting. In New York, factional politics rather than popular discontent led to a convention in 1821, but once the convention assembled voting reform became a major topic of debate. James Kent, an eminent jurist, fearfully but unsuccessfully opposed a proposition to "bow before the idol of universal suffrage" and the "annihila[tion] . . . of property distinctions." The constitution drafted by the convention and approved by the voters gave the vote to white males who paid taxes, served in the militia or as firemen, or worked on the highways—which in practice meant just about all of them. Blacks could vote, too, but they had to own property. The proportion of adult white males eligible to vote for governor jumped from 33% to 84%.[5]

Notwithstanding the reduction of property qualifications for voting and eventual attainment of universal white manhood suffrage, achieving equal representation in state legislatures sometimes proved difficult. We have already noted the significance of the apportionment issue in Virginia and Rhode Island. In Maryland, too, where the property qualification for voting was eliminated in 1802, malapportionment remained a major source of demands for constitutional reform from 1830 through the constitutional convention of 1850–51.

Suffrage and apportionment reforms served the twin goals of equal rights and majority rule. Jefferson complained in the 1820s that Virginia's existing constitution was opposed "to the principle of equal political rights, refusing to all but freeholders [landowners] any participation in the natural right of self-government." Denying the majority of freeholders the right to vote, he wrote, was a "usurpation of the minority over the majority." Andrew Jackson, the hero of the common man, personally fostered political egalitarianism. The "first principle" of the American political system, he declared, is "that the majority is to govern." He believed that "[t]he duties of all public officers" could be made "so plain and simple that men of intelligence may readily qualify themselves for their performance." Men might not enjoy equal talents, education, or wealth, but they were entitled to equal protection of the laws. If government "would confine itself to equal protection, and, as Heaven does its rains, shower its favors alike on the high and the low, the rich and the poor," Jackson said, "it would be an unqualified blessing."

The political philosophy of majority rule and white equality made up the positive component of Jacksonian Democracy—what Jacksonian Democracy stood *for*. But there was also a negative component that came to the fore only after Jackson left the White House. This element consisted of an antipathy toward government that Jackson himself did not share. Jackson believed in a government that was simple and frugal, but he did not view government as a necessary evil. Indeed, as we have just seen, he described government properly administered as "an unqualified blessing." "There are no necessary evils in government," said Jackson. "Its evils exist only in its abuses."

Nevertheless, during the Jacksonian era there arose a more hostile view of government. Abuses of various kinds contributed to this attitude, but none more than the real or imagined use of governmental power to benefit private interests at the expense of the public—what today would be denounced as "crony capitalism." At first, public hostility focused on banks. The Second Bank of the United States, chartered by Congress in 1816, encouraged the anger by a reckless expansion of credit that contributed to the financial panic of 1819 and the depression that followed. State-chartered banks were often worse.

In the first half of the nineteenth century banking corporations—indeed, all corporations—received their legal authority to organize and function through the passage of special legislative acts. If a group of individuals wanted to form a corporation for banking, manufacturing, literary, or any other purpose, it had to get the state legislature to enact a law granting a corporate charter. The law would include the rights and powers of the corporation. In the case of a bank, the law might require the bank to have a specified amount of paid-in capital before engaging in business, authorize the bank to issue promissory notes (which, it was understood, would circulate as if they were money), and reserve to the state the right to purchase a certain amount of the bank's stock. If the corporation's purpose was to build a turnpike from one town to another, the statute might authorize the corporation to lay out the road through other people's lands, take stone and timber from adjoining property, and charge tolls once the road was completed. Legislatures devoted an enormous amount of time to the enactment of such special laws. When the profusion of special laws, with their grants of "exclusive privileges," coincided with hard times, people questioned whether government could be trusted to act in the public interest.

Turnpikes were a form of "internal improvement," as were canals, railroads, bridges, and projects to enhance harbors and make rivers more readily navigable. Internal improvements were the economic development schemes of their day. State and county governments eagerly financed the construction of turnpikes, canals, and railroads, both publicly and privately owned, with taxpayer money. States and counties sold millions of dollars' worth of bonds to domestic and foreign investors. Politicians and corporations often pitched the projects with the promise that the improvements would produce more than enough revenue to pay off the bonds, so that the public would get the benefits of the projects tax-free.

Eighteenth-century Americans probably could not have imagined the vast scope of the internal improvement projects that state legislatures in the nineteenth century would approve. But there was in fact a long tradition of governmental promotion of economic development in America. Colonial assemblies had offered loans, land grants, tax abatements, and other incentives to various types of enterprises, including sawmills, fulling mills, iron works, and, above all, gristmills. Over half the colonies adopted mill acts to encourage the construction of gristmills.

With their waterwheels, millstones, gears, and shafts, gristmills were complicated and expensive enterprises. The better ones usually required a dam to build a head of water sufficient to turn the wheel, gates and sluices to control the volume and direction of the flow, and a tailrace to direct the water back into the stream at maximum speed after turning the wheel. The miller needed a building big enough to house the machinery and to collect, clean, and dry the meal or flour. And he had to repair or replace virtually the entire wheel, except for the main shaft, every five to ten years. In short, a gristmill required capital and expertise beyond the ability of most early settlers to provide.

The miller also needed enough land on both sides of a stream to contain the mill, race, and dam. As the demand for meal and flour grew, the law changed to meet obstacles that stood in the way of construction of more and bigger mills. In Virginia, would-be millers sometimes had trouble acquiring both sides of stream banks to construct their dams. As the legislature put it in 1667, "diverse persons" would willingly erect mills "for the grinding of corne" at "convenient places . . . if not obstructed by the perverse-nesse of some persons not permitting others, though not willing themselves to promote so publique a good." To remedy this situation, the lawmakers granted millers eminent-domain rights. A prospective miller who owned one bank of a stream could take an acre on the opposite bank from an owner unwilling to sell, with compensation to be determined by two commissioners appointed to appraise the land. The Virginia law became a model for other southern colonies.

In New England, milldams often flooded the property of other landowners or interfered with their milling operations. Inundated landowners sued for injunctions or damages, threatening the continued operation of the offending mills. To protect millers from repeated and ruinous lawsuits, the Massachusetts General Court in 1714 limited the remedy for such flooding to annual damages to be determined by a jury. In effect, the law gave millers eminent domain rights by allowing them to use the property of others, without consent, in return for monetary compensation. Just as Virginia's law of 1667 became a model for the South, the Mass-achusetts law served as a model for New England.

Even as flour production grew into a big, profitable business not in need of public assistance, Americans found it hard to shake the notion that government had an important role to play in both regulating and promoting commerce. Virginia amended its mill act to grant eminent domain privileges not just for gristmills but also for any "other machine or engine useful to the public." The governor of Massachusetts wanted to extend the principles of that state's act to textile mills and other "labour saving machines." The Mississippi Territory gave eminent domain powers to all "useful water-works." The disruption of trade before and during the War of 1812 led to additional governmental efforts to encourage manufacturing, including, at the national level, the enactment of a protective tariff and the creation of the Second Bank of the United States in 1816.

State legislatures also started granting more and more corporate charters. The New York legislature granted 165 charters to manufacturing corporations between 1808 and 1815. After the war, writes an economic historian, some state legislatures "appear to have adopted the view that the chartering of domestic manufacturing concerns was required by patriotism."[6] State and local governments, long accustomed to fostering roadbuilding and canal construction, built on that tradition by offering land grants, eminent domain rights, loans of money or credit, and stock subscriptions to turnpike and canal companies.

While all this public promotion of private enterprise was going on, the seeds of an opposing point of view began to sprout. The Revolution had taught Americans that government must no longer be the extension of private interests, as it had been under King George III. Public power could not be used for the benefit of special interests or private individuals. Corporate charters, which had once been seen as ways to limit royal power, came to be viewed as privileges that protected corporations from the power of popular government. The year 1776 not only saw the birth of a new nation imbued with this revolutionary ideology, it also witnessed the publication of Adam Smith's *The Wealth of Nations*. Smith criticized export bounties, price regulations, restrictions on trade, and other forms of governmental intervention in the economy. Thomas Jefferson praised *The Wealth of Nations* as the best book ever published on political economy.

These two opposing views clashed dramatically in the long fight over the Boston and Roxbury Mill Dam Company, incorporated in 1814. The Boston city fathers, together with private businessmen, conceived a plan to remake the urban landscape. The company, chartered with the purpose of creating waterpower for industrial development, proposed to construct a huge basin and reservoirs and a series of dams and roadways to control the tide in Boston's Back Bay. The project would connect peninsular Boston to other parts of the mainland and change the face of the city. This was promotion on a grand scale. According to one of the company's principals, the project would produce eighty-one power sites for mills of every description. The company's charter authorized the company to charge tolls for the use of its roadways when it reached a certain level of power production. The charter also established a procedure to assess damages when private parties claimed injury as a result of the company's dams, canals, raceways, and other constructions. However, it did not require that any particular type of mill be built, or that the mills serve the public generally, or that tolls be limited.

Not everyone had a sanguine view of the project. Benjamin Austin, a popular writer and newspaperman, described the project as another in the promoters' series of speculative enterprises that benefited themselves but left others destitute. The company's mills, he charged, would monopolize the city's bread supply, pollute the air, and depreciate land elsewhere in the city. In short, the company's charter was a grant of exclusive privileges to private speculators, with no evidence that the speculation would be of public utility.

The project went forward in fits and starts and proved to be a financial failure as well as an environmental nuisance. It also resulted in repeated conflicts between the Boston and Roxbury Mill Dam Company and landowners bordering the proposed basin. The company and most of the landowners compromised their differences in 1826. Some landowners, however, rejected the compromise, and in 1832 the company brought suit against a man named Newman, charging that he had interfered with flowage from a gristmill by filling in a portion of the basin for the construction of his house. Newman countered that the company's charter was unconstitutional. Newman claimed that the company's purpose "was not a matter of public convenience and necessity, but of private speculation." The court did not agree. It saw a "direct public interest and benefit" in the creation of "immense perpetual mill power" and in the employment of "great numbers of citizens" by the factories.

By the time Mr. Newman lost his case, there was a rumbling among democratically inclined thinkers against economic development schemes fostered by government. In Philadelphia, Condy

Raguet published a journal called *The Free Trade Advocate* sporting the motto "laissez-nous faire" (let us alone). In New York, journalist William Leggett also wished for the day when legislators would be governed by the maxim "let us alone." Men such as Raguet and Leggett objected to any governmental encouragement or grant of privileges "to any particular class of industry, or any select bodies of men, inasmuch as all classes of industry and all men are equally important to the general welfare, and equally entitled to protection." When government gave out favors, they said, the rich would always get the lion's share, and government would become their tool.

Until the bubble burst, though, most Americans remained enthralled with the idea that government should promote economic development. The great success of New York's Erie Canal fueled the promotional spirit. New Yorkers had long dreamt of a waterway that would connect Lake Erie with the Hudson River. The project was too big for private capital, and the federal government refused to lend its support, so the state decided to go it alone. The Erie Canal opened in 1825 and immediately produced a profit for the state. It proved an economic boon for the whole country along its path and for New York City, the port at the mouth of the Hudson. The success of the Erie Canal inspired other state and local governments to aid private canal companies through loans, loan guarantees, stock subscriptions, and grants of eminent domain privileges. When railroads became technologically feasible, governments aided them, too. People all over the country believed that their counties and towns would thrive if only they had better connections with the rest of the world.

To provide currency and credit for the booming economy, states chartered new banks by the dozen. Banks had a shady reputation. Every time a financial panic or recession occurred, banks received much of the blame. Sometimes they deserved it. There was no official paper money in those days, and many places suffered shortages of gold and silver coins. Banks made up the deficiency by issuing banknotes, which were promises to pay in coin when the notes were brought in for redemption. The bewildering variety of such notes, inadequate banking regulation, and the shaky foundations of many banks made it hard for people to know the value of the notes they held and used. Not surprisingly, when citizens complained about the special privileges that lawmakers granted to corporations, they usually had banks in mind.

Andrew Jackson hated banks. His proudest achievement as president was "killing the monster," as he called the Second Bank of the United States, by vetoing the act of Congress that renewed its charter. A believer in strict construction of the United States Constitution, Jackson also vetoed a federal internal improvements bill because he thought it included projects that lay within the sole jurisdiction of the states. However, notwithstanding his subsequent gripe about the "log rolling system of internal improvements," his veto message noted the "laudable zeal" with which many states were pursuing the "enlightened policy" of constructing roads and canals. Jackson apparently did not object to internal improvements constructed by or with the assistance of the states.

Nor did most other Democrats during Jackson's presidency. The zeal for internal improvements was bipartisan. In Jackson's home state of Tennessee, where the president was immensely popular, a constitutional convention in 1834 produced a document with the following internal improvements clause: "A well-regulated system of internal improvements is calculated to develop the resources of the State, and to promote the happiness and prosperity of her citizens; therefore, it ought to be encouraged by the General Assembly." The first constitution of Michigan, a Democratic territory, adopted that same year, also required the government to encourage internal improvements. It placed upon the legislature the duty "to make provision by law for ascertaining the proper objects of improvement, in relation to roads, canals and navigable waters."

The general public enthusiasm for government promotionalism might have continued unabated but for the Panic of 1837 and the ensuing economic depression. Both major political parties, Democratic and Whig, rode the internal improvements bandwagon, at least when it came to state and local as opposed to federal sponsorship. The depression caused people to reconsider. Many of the projects failed, some spectacularly, leaving taxpayers to pay off the bonds issued to finance them. Public debt skyrocketed. So did business failures and unemployment. When Illinois stopped work on a canal, the towns along its route emptied out. Illinoisans, reported writer James K. Paulding, were "precipitated from the summit of hope to the lowest abyss of debt and depression." Contemporary observers related scenes of desolation and despair all over the country. People grew disenchanted with government-sponsored development programs. They saw in them poor planning and oversight, political favoritism, legislative logrolling, and plunder. The cry arose to get government out of economic affairs.

The Panic also sharpened differences between the Whigs and Democrats. American political parties have always been loose alliances of diverse groups, with no official ideology and with internal inconsistencies based on regional differences. Nevertheless, after the Panic, mainstream Democrats, already hostile toward banks and their paper money, turned against corporations generally and against governmental interference in the economy. "The less government interference with private pursuits, the better for the general prosperity," President Martin Van Buren, a Democrat, told Congress in 1837. Governmental attempts to aid and regulate private enterprise, he declared, had always proved injurious and inevitably resulted in the bestowal of special favors upon individuals or classes, leading to well-founded complaints of "partiality, injustice, and oppression." In the first issue of the *Democratic Review*, published a few months after the Panic of 1837 threw the nation's economy into turmoil, editor John L. O'Sullivan called "a strong and active democratic *government* . . . an evil, differing only in degree and mode of operation, and not in nature, from a strong despotism." Because majorities could not more be trusted with power than minorities, the "best government is that which governs least."

Whigs disagreed. Government had higher objects than simply national defense and the maintenance of order, said a Whig governor. Government had an obligation "to foster and protect all the great interests of the country"; to see that "the laws are framed with special reference to the wants, employments and necessities of the people; and to aid the enterprise, industry, and interests of the community." "[O]ur philosophy," wrote a leading Whig editor, "regards a Government with hope and confidence, as an agency of the community through which vast and beneficent ends may be accomplished," while radical Democrats viewed government "with distrust and aversion, as an agency mainly of corruption, oppression, and robbery."

Hostility toward government in the wake of the Panic was the negative component of Jacksonian Democracy. Reflecting an attitude that spread well beyond Ohio, Buckeyes referred to the state's Loan Law of 1837, which required the state to give loans to railroad, canal, and turnpike companies, as the Plunder Law. People began to see a need for constitutional restraints on government. Most early state constitutions imposed few limits on what government could do. They had bills of rights, of course, but when it came to taxing and spending, the checks on government were political in nature: broad suffrage, short terms of office, frequent elections. If the voters didn't like what their lawmakers were doing, they could throw the rascals out. But the Panic deepened the widespread feeling that constitutional restraints were needed to prevent abuses of power.

It is doubtful that economic difficulties alone would have produced all those midcentury constitutional conventions; depressions gave way to recoveries, and Americans' desire for promotionalism would reassert itself. But unhappy citizens had other complaints, too. State legislatures spent too much time passing laws for the special benefit of individuals or small groups of people. State court systems could not handle growing caseloads. Many important public officers were appointed by governors and legislators rather than elected by the people. Population growth, the rise of cities, and gerrymandering had led to the unfair apportionment of legislatures. The public schools were abysmal. When economic woes combined with other, more enduring causes, constitutional conventions, usually dominated by Democrats, proved more than willing to impose constitutional limitations on the power of lawmakers to do harm. People simply did not trust the government.

Distrust led to an insistence on greater accountability and transparency in government. The Panic of 1837 and the depression that followed aroused tremendous hostility toward state legislatures that had embarked on extravagant internal improvement programs and plunged the states into debt. The people themselves bore much of the blame because they had clamored for all those roads, canals, and railroads in the first place. Nevertheless, they expected their elected representatives to use good judgment in implementing the people's wishes and to exercise their powers in an honorable manner. When the Panic exploded their dreams, the people's complaints involved more than the financial risks the legislators had taken. The people groused not only about *what* the legislatures did but also about *how* they did it.

For a modern analogy, think of the federal Patient Protection and Affordable Care Act of 2010—Obamacare. When the bill was in Congress, opponents complained vociferously about the huge impact it would have on the economy, about the program's likely cost, and about the accretion of power it would give to federal regulators, but they also condemned the process by which the bill got enacted. Supporters in Congress played fast and loose with the rules. Senators gutted an unrelated House bill and replaced its substance with Obamacare in order to move it along. To prevent a filibuster by opponents, the majority made questionable use of the process by which different versions of bills passed by the House and Senate are reconciled. A House Democrat conceded, "we make [the rules] up as we go along." The bill's backers bought votes by promising special benefits to particular states and institutions. Opponents dubbed the best-known deals the "Cornhusker Kickback" and the "Louisiana Purchase." The Kickback aroused such furious condemnation that the senator who requested it asked for its removal from the bill. But other, lesser-known provisions, such as one called "Protection of Second Amendment Gun Rights," remained hidden in the gargantuan bill. House Speaker Nancy Pelosi's notorious statement that "[w]e have to pass the bill so that you can find out what is in it," although often misconstrued, no doubt reflected the reality that many in Congress had little detailed knowledge of the bill's contents. The manner in which Congress passed Obamacare encouraged a widely held public perception that the whole legislative process was corrupt.

State legislatures in the middle of the nineteenth century were no purer than Congress is today. As early as 1804, the Ohio governor complained about the "low, cunning, trifling, intrigueing conduct of a few restless, ambitious Spirits in our Legislature," while others described the lawmakers as inexperienced, ignorant, obstinate time-wasters. Time did not improve the members' image. Annual sessions and frequent elections made the lawmakers theoretically accountable to the voters, but it was hard to keep track of legislators' activities on a day-to-day basis.

Early state constitutions gave legislators plenty of leeway for wheeling, dealing, and intrigue by imposing few procedural rules. Here, for example, are the rules of procedure contained in Ohio's 1802 constitution, the first state constitution in the Old Northwest:

- two-thirds of each house constitute a quorum;
- each house must keep a journal of its proceedings and record the votes of the members on any question if requested by at least two members;
- any two members of a house may protest any act or resolution and have the reasons for their protest published in the journal;
- sessions must be open to the public except when secrecy is required;
- bills may originate in either house but may be altered, amended, or rejected by the other house;
- every bill must be read on three different days in each house, unless, "in case of urgency," the members dispense with the rule by a three-fourths vote;
- every bill that passes both houses must be signed by the speakers of both houses.

The constitution also allowed each house to adopt its own rules of procedure. The state legislatures of the Old Northwest inherited a long tradition of procedure from Parliament, Congress, and the Northwest Territory. However, both the constitutional and the legislative rules left lots of room for activity that was, or at least could be construed as being, unsavory, and enforcement of the rules was largely up to the legislatures themselves. A notorious example of legislative sneakiness occurred in 1795. Speculators had their eyes on huge tracts of land in western territories (present-day Alabama and Mississippi) claimed by Georgia. To induce the Georgia legislature to transfer the state's claims to them, the speculators liberally distributed money and land to lawmakers and other influential men. Soon the General Assembly passed a bill entitled "An Act for the Payment of the late State Troops." No one, including inattentive legislators, who looked just at the bill's title would know that the bill sold thirty-five million acres of land to the speculators for $500,000. The public outrage that erupted when the truth came out caused the legislature to rescind the deal, which in turn led to one of the most important U.S. Supreme Court decisions of the nineteenth century.

The uninformative title was just one problem with the Georgia law. Another was the fact that the law dealt with two unrelated subjects, the payment of state militiamen and the sale of western lands. The idea that every bill should address just one subject went all the way back to ancient Rome. British authorities repeatedly warned colonial governments to stick to the rule. In 1702, for example, Queen Anne instructed the governor of New Jersey to avoid "intermixing in one and the same act, such things as have no proper relation to each other." But the colonies continued to flout the rule. The states thus inherited two traditions, one of prohibiting the "intermixing" of different subjects in the same act, and the other of doing just that. Lax observance of the rule gave lawmakers opportunities to tack unpopular measures onto popular ones or, as in the case of the Georgia law, to slip extraneous provisions by careless or harried colleagues.

A related issue involved the amendment of existing laws by referring to their titles or to parts of their text. Again, the Affordable Care Act provides a modern illustration of the problem. Here is just a portion of Section 1562(a) of the Act:

APPLICABILITY. — Section 2735 of the Public Health Service Act (42 U.S.C. 300gg-21), as so redesignated by section 1001(4), is amended —

(1) by striking subsection (a);

(2) in subsection (b) —

(A) in paragraph (1), by striking "1 through 3" and inserting "1 and 2"; and

(B) in paragraph (2) —

(i) in subparagraph (A), by striking "subparagraph (D)" and inserting "subparagraph (D) or (E)";

(ii) by striking "1 through 3" and inserting "1 and 2"; and

(iii) by adding at the end the following:

"(E) ELECTION NOT APPLICABLE. — The election described in subparagraph (A) shall not be available with respect to the provisions of subpart 1."

Without seeing the full text of Section 2735 of the Public Health Service Act, the law being amended by Section 1562(a) of the Affordable Care Act, can anyone not already familiar with the law see what Congress actually did here? This type of amendment is not unique to Obamacare. It is typical of federal laws. Nor was it prompted by a desire to hide what Congress was doing. The Affordable Care Act is nearly a thousand pages long. If the complete text of all the sections of law amended by the Act had been included, the Act would have filled a truck. But this amendment by reference certainly obscures the law.

In the nineteenth century, few laws ran on for hundreds of pages. Nevertheless, legislatures often amended existing statutes by using references as shortcuts. For example, one section of an 1845 Missouri militia law read: "The second section of the first article, and so much of the remainder of the act, entitled 'an act to regulate, govern and discipline the militia of the State of Missouri,' approved March 27, 1845, as is inconsistent with the provisions of this act, is hereby repealed." A New York school law of 1849 provided: "Section 6 of the act entitled, 'An act establishing free schools throughout the state,['] passed March 26, 1849, is hereby amended by striking out the word 'second,' in the last line of said section, and inserting the word 'third' in lieu thereof, and the said section shall be amended accordingly in the printed copies of said act when published by the secretary of state." "Amendatory statutes" of this type, said one court, were sometimes enacted "in terms so blind" that the lawmakers themselves did not understand their effect; the public, unable to make "the necessary examination and comparison," simply had no clue. The court insinuated that sometimes legislatures deliberately amended the law in such a manner in order to mislead the public.

The average citizen probably knew little about the use and abuse of bill-drafting technicalities. He was more likely to get worked up over the impropriety of logrolling. Logrolling was a form of legislative deal making that often served legitimate purposes, but, possibly as a result of the collapse of internal improvement schemes after the Panic of 1837, it acquired a bad reputation. Here is how U.S. senator James Buchanan explained the phenomenon in 1842:

> One [legislator] has a measure of mere local advantage to carry, which ought, if at all, to be accomplished by individual enterprise, and which could not pass if it stood alone. He finds that he cannot accomplish his object, if he relies only upon its merits. He finds that other members have other local objects at heart, none of which would receive the support of a majority if separately considered. These members, then, form a combination sufficiently powerful to carry the whole; and thus twenty measures may be adopted, no one of which separately could have obtained a respectable vote.

Buchanan blamed logrolling for the internal improvements debacles from which the states were still reeling. As we will see, he had good reason to do so.

Logrolling and legislation by stealth—misleading bill titles, multiple subjects in one bill, amendments by reference, all of which could be used to conceal the true nature of legislative acts—

all related to the lawmaking process. But nineteenth-century state legislatures did more than pass laws. One of their chief functions was to elect public officers—judges, state auditors and treasurers, in some states even governors. People occasionally accused legislators of abusing their power to elect public officials by putting themselves or their personal or political friends into office. But even if the selection process had been simon-pure, the indirect election of so many important officials would have run counter to the tendencies of Jacksonian Democracy. An Ohio legislative committee asserted in 1834 that the people's natural right to "appoint their own agents" was "essential to the very existence of a free government." Indiana and Michigan provided for the election of some lower-court judges before 1837. Mississippi opted for the election of all judges in 1832. By the early 1830s, Ohioans were electing justices of the peace as well as county prosecutors, sheriffs, coroners, recorders, and surveyors. It was harder to achieve the popular election of officials at the state than at the local level. State constitutions generally gave to the legislatures the power of choosing higher-court judges, secretaries of state, and other important public officers, and the constitutions were hard to amend. As the distrust of state legislatures rose after the Panic of 1837, though, so did demands for constitutional conventions and for the popular election of public officials.

The turn to constitutional conventions as a means of redress was natural. After the Revolution, the United States found itself in possession of a vast, unorganized domain east of the Mississippi River. With the Louisiana Purchase of 1803 and the subsequent acquisition of Florida, the United States' extensive holdings spread to the west and south. There were in addition the independent republic of Vermont and Massachusetts' District of Maine. Fourteen new states entered the Union from these lands before 1840; all but Vermont held constitutional conventions in preparation for statehood, and Vermont had its own history of constitutional conventions before joining the Union in 1791. A fifteenth state, Florida, also held a convention before 1840 as a preliminary step toward statehood, although Florida did not gain admission until 1845. Furthermore, more than a dozen states held post-admission conventions before 1840 to revise their constitutions. Many of these constitutions provided for no amending process other than a convention.

The constitutional convention movement of the 1840s formally began in 1841 when the Louisiana legislature passed a law calling for a popular referendum on the holding of a convention. The law set forth a list of subjects to be considered by the convention: qualifications for suffrage, apportionment of the state legislature, the method of choosing the governor, the jurisdiction and meeting places of the state supreme court, and a territorial issue. Because the voters had to approve a convention at two successive elections, the convention did not actually meet until August 1844. In the meantime, the New Jersey legislature scheduled an election for delegates to a constitutional convention in 1844, and the territorial legislature of Iowa put the question of calling a convention before the voters. The New Jersey convention assembled in May 1844; the Iowa convention, having been approved by the voters, met in August.

Popular outrage against legislative profligacy did not drive the constitutional convention movement in any of these jurisdictions. Nor did Jacksonian ideology. Nevertheless, Jacksonian ideas found their way into the constitutions drafted by all three conventions. The Louisiana convention, almost evenly divided between Whig and Democratic delegates, strayed beyond the bounds set by the legislature. The delegates prohibited state debt over $100,000 unless the legislature specified the purpose for the debt and created a tax to pay it off. They also barred the state from purchasing corporate stock; prohibited the incorporation of banks; banned special acts of incorporation; outlawed the pledge of the state's faith for the payment of individual or corporate obligations; and limited grants of monopoly or "exclusive privileges" to twenty years. In New Jersey, where the call for a convention had bipartisan support, the delegates established a state debt ceiling and prohibited the state from lending its credit to private companies or individuals. Both conventions required that every act of the legislature deal with only one subject, which had to be expressed in the act's title. The purpose of this provision, as expressed in the

New Jersey constitution, was to "avoid improper influences which may result from intermixing in one and the same act such things as have no proper relation to each other"—in other words, to prevent lawmakers from sneaking things into acts without proper notice. Both conventions also did away with property qualifications for voting and provided, for the first time in those states, for the untrammeled popular election of governors.

In Iowa, the convention arose from the contest over statehood, which Democrats generally supported and many Whigs opposed. The draft constitution of 1844 incorporated many ideas cherished by the dominant Democrats: a debt ceiling, a prohibition of state ownership of corporate stock and of providing aid or credit to private parties, limits on corporate charters, and so on. The voters rejected the constitution, largely because of the state borders established by Congress.

Despite its failure at the polls, the Iowa constitution of 1844 portended a new direction for state constitutions. Its radical Jacksonian tenor would characterize most of the constitutions adopted during the convention surge of the next few years. Consider the unusual case of Texas, an independent republic since 1836 and a Mexican state before then. Texas held a constitutional convention in contemplation of American statehood in 1845. The constitutions of Mexican Texas and the Republic of Texas granted suffrage to adult white males, provided for the popular election of local officials, and prohibited monopolies and banks. These features all reappeared in the 1845 constitution. Texas had struggled with debt during its period of independence, but due to military expenditures and not internal improvements.[7] The new constitution, though, not only set a state debt limit, it required a two-thirds vote of the legislature to authorize state borrowing or to create a private corporation, required that property be taxed according to its value, barred the state from partnering with corporations through the ownership of stock or other property, and required that every law embrace only one object expressed in its title. The constitution did not include a provision of its 1833 predecessor that expressly authorized the legislature to establish a system of internal improvements.

Missouri, too, held a constitutional convention in 1845. Complaints about the court system and a desire to fill more public offices by popular election instead of appointment contributed to the movement for a convention, but the chief ground of discontent was unequal representation in the state legislature. (The constitution required that each county have at least one state representative but limited the size of the house of representatives to one hundred. The wholesale creation of new counties with small populations produced the inequality.) The draft constitution adopted by the convention went far beyond these issues. It eliminated a clause stating that internal improvements "shall forever be encouraged" and prohibited state ownership of corporate stock or other corporate property. It also retained the anti-bank bias of the current constitution, imposed a strict state debt limit, provided that the legislature could repeal corporate charters, and made shareholders individually liable for corporate debts. The constitution failed at the polls. Judge Robert William Wells, a leading Democrat and president of the convention, blamed the defeat on the opposition of "Bank men," but a Whig newspaper complained of other defects in the proposed constitution, particularly the apportionment provisions. Missourians soon addressed the judicial and representation issues with constitutional amendments.

In 1846 Iowans tried again. All of the Jacksonian features of the constitution proposed in 1844 reappeared, except for a provision imposing unlimited liability on shareholders for corporate debts. The chief differences between the 1844 and 1846 documents had to do with the structure of the executive and judicial branches of state government and the organization of counties. Pursuant to an act of Congress, the boundary question was left to the U.S. Supreme Court to resolve. Iowans approved the new constitution in a close vote.

While the Iowa conclave was going on, a constitutional convention met in New York. Constitutional amendments had moved the state further along the path of democracy since the 1821 convention, but dissatisfaction with state government had risen. The judicial system could not keep up with the growth in population, business, and litigation. Special legislation, especially the granting of charters to banks and other corporations, took up most of the legislature's time. Farmers protested New York's antiquated system of feudal land tenures by launching the sometimes violent Anti-Rent War. And public debt, most of it due to the costs of the state's canal system and to the lending of state credit to private corporations, had gotten out of control. Whigs who wanted to break the hold of a Democratic faction on patronage teamed up with radical Democrats to put the convention issue on the ballot. The voters approved the call by a large majority.

The convention, dominated by radical Democrats, instituted a debt ceiling, above which all debts had to be funded by a tax approved by a popular referendum; prohibited most special acts of incorporation, including all special acts incorporating banks; adopted the one-subject rule for legislation; made major state executive and judicial offices elective; confirmed the statutory abolition of feudal land tenures; and revamped the court system. The proposed constitution, which the voters ratified by a huge margin, embodied "the emergent ideology of laissez-faire individualism."[8] Thus was the table set for the constitutional conventions in the Old Northwest.

"Upper Territories of the United States"

Published in Baltimore, ca. 1816, by mapmaker Fielding Lucas Jr.

Courtesy Barry Lawrence Ruderman Antique Maps, www.RareMaps.com,
used by permission, as with other maps reproduced in this volume

3

The Northwest Territory and its States

The end of the American Revolution brought international recognition of American sovereignty over an area stretching from Pennsylvania to the Mississippi River and from the Ohio River to present-day Manitoba. That vast region would be called the Northwest Territory.

Eager to promote the settlement of the territory in an orderly fashion, Congress, in one of its last acts under the Articles of Confederation, passed the Northwest Ordinance to provide a framework of government. While the Ordinance guaranteed individual rights and promised republican government and equality with the original states in the future, it did not provide for government by the consent of the governed, at least not initially and not entirely thereafter. Congress appointed all the chief territorial officials: the governor, the secretary, and three judges, all five of whom had to be substantial landowners. Congress also named all general officers of the militia. The governor in turn appointed magistrates and other local officials and militia officers below the rank of general. He also had the power to lay out counties and townships, subject to subsequent alteration by the territorial legislature, which consisted of the governor and the three judges appointed by Congress. The legislators had no power to make laws, but they could adopt any laws of the original thirteen states that they thought appropriate for the territory.

The Ordinance looked forward to a more democratic government when the territory would have five thousand free male inhabitants. Even then, though, the government would resemble that of a British colony. A house of representatives would be elected by men who met the residency and property qualifications, but Congress would still choose the governor, secretary, and other officers, as well as a five-member legislative council from a list of ten nominees selected by the representatives. The governor, legislative council, and house of representatives together would make up the General Assembly. This body would be able to pass laws, but the governor would have an absolute veto and the power to dissolve the General Assembly at will.

The undemocratic nature of the territory's political arrangements displeased many of the settlers. Pressure for representative government built throughout the 1790s. No sooner had a newspaper appeared in November 1793 than a disgruntled reader complained of "the oppressive hand of a legislature, in the formation or organization of which he was not consulted." Secretary Winthrop Sargent's arbitrary rule in Governor Arthur St. Clair's absence provoked like cries of "tyranny and despotism." In the popular calls that led to the legislative session of 1795, demands for law reform were mixed with criticism of the tyrannical government of four unelected men. The clamor for representative government spread with the rapid growth of population after General Anthony Wayne decisively defeated the Indians at the Battle of Fallen Timbers in 1794. In 1798 St. Clair, believing that the territory had the requisite number of inhabitants for the establishment of a general assembly, set the third Monday in December as the date for the election of representatives.

The Northwest Ordinance set property qualifications of two hundred acres to serve in the house of representatives and fifty acres to vote. For every five hundred free male inhabitants, there would be one representative, to a maximum of twenty-five, after which the legislature would fix the number and proportion of members. St. Clair interpreted these provisions liberally, so that town dwellers who had houses but not much land qualified to vote if they possessed an estate equal in value to the average fifty acres of land in the same county. Even so, the franchise was more restricted than in any of the states.

The Indiana, Michigan, Illinois, and Wisconsin territories that subsequently would be established in the Old Northwest followed more or less the same pattern of government as the original Northwest Territory. Federally appointed governors and judges would give way to popularly elected legislatures as the territories grew, but the inhabitants often felt constrained by their federal overlords. Notwithstanding the financial benefits that Congress afforded, the majority of the people in the territories seemed eager to take the reins of government into their own hands. The difficulties faced by the Northwest Territory's first elected representatives in getting together for their initial legislative session showed the need for internal improvements in the vast, sparsely settled province. St. Clair called the session for January 22, 1799, in Cincinnati, but delegates from distant areas—present-day Michigan, Illinois, and Indiana—found that traveling hundreds of miles through the wilderness in winter was no easy task. Even the members from Marietta, in present-day Ohio, had trouble getting to the session. They trudged through long stretches of dreary woods bearing no signs of human habitation, camping at night in the winter cold, swimming their horses across streams, traveling no roads except bridle paths or Indian trails. The session did not open until February 4.

Jacob Burnet, one of the most important public figures in the Northwest Territory, illustrated the perils of travel with a description of a journey he took in the fall of 1800. Burnet was one of a half-dozen lawyers who, along with Judge John Cleves Symmes, set out on horseback from Cincinnati for a court session in Marietta. Traveling through a thinly inhabited wilderness, the group crossed the Hocking River near today's Athens, where they found a cabin. The occupants directed them to a path several miles away that would take them directly to Marietta. Symmes and company located the path late that afternoon, as clouds gathered. Soon night came on, and the men had trouble staying on course in the dark. Nevertheless, they decided to forge ahead, taking turns leading on foot, feeling but not seeing the path.

Sometime after midnight, Burnet, leading his horse, strayed off the trail and stepped into a small ravine. Frightened by the jolt, the horse recoiled and thereby kept Burnet from falling. After Burnet found his footing, the group recovered the path, which led downhill to a creek. On the opposite bank stood a cabin where, after repeatedly assuring the inhabitants that they were peaceable folk, they gained shelter for the night. The next morning, a twelve-mile ride took the men to Marietta. On their return journey, the party discovered that Burnet had barely missed dropping off a steep cliff into the treetops below.

As Burnet later recalled, "privation and exposure, and often with great personal danger," always attended such excursions. The judges of the Northwest Territory had trouble holding court at the required times throughout their immense jurisdiction. The "vast distances" to be traveled, through unsettled country "overrun, at times, with hostile savages," without roads and with unnavigable streams, made it difficult all year. In the winter, ice made water travel even more dangerous. One territorial judge died while running the rapids of the Big Beaver River in a canoe.

Burnet belonged to the Federalist Party, one of two political parties to emerge in the 1790s. Federalists believed in a strong national government and an executive authority with real power. Their opponents, the Jeffersonian Republicans, remained skeptical of both, even after the adoption of the Bill of Rights in 1791 allayed some of their fears. Federalists distrusted democracy, a sentiment strengthened by their abhorrence of the French Revolution; Republicans believed in the virtue and good sense of the people, and for a long time they viewed the French Revolution as a continuation of the American. Many Federalists favored commercial development; for Republicans, the ideal society consisted of sturdy yeomen. These are generalizations, of course. Federalists John Adams and Alexander Hamilton disagreed over the advantages of a commercial republic, and Republican Thomas Jefferson knew that the people could be corrupted, especially if they congregated in cities. But for the most part, Federalists favored energetic government by the "better sort," while Republicans leaned toward agrarian democracy and limited government.

The Federalists and Republicans of the 1790s lacked the organizational structure that later came to characterize parties. The physical and constitutional situation of the Northwest Territory retarded party development. Except for a few clusters in Marietta, Cincinnati, and Chillicothe, the population was scattered through an enormous wilderness. With no popular assembly before 1799 and governmental power concentrated in the hands of four federally appointed officials, the people had little opportunity to express themselves politically. Practical considerations also blurred political divisions. Frontier farmers who constituted a natural Republican constituency appreciated the protection the federal government afforded against Indian depredations.

St. Clair's power of patronage and sectional rivalries, particularly over the location of the future capital, also inhibited partisan organization. The candidates for the house of representatives in 1798 did not contest the election along party lines, and the house submitted to Congress a mixed list of nominees for the legislative council. There was, nevertheless, a subtle sense of antagonism in the house toward the Federalist St. Clair. One representative wrote, "our Governor is cloathed with all the power of a British Nabob."

St. Clair polarized the factions and radicalized the opposition at the end of the first territorial General Assembly by vetoing eleven of thirty laws passed. In his message to the legislature St. Clair displayed a distinct lack of diplomacy by bluntly insisting on his prerogative. Some of the governor's opponents now argued that only statehood could rid them of arbitrary, undemocratic rule. But St. Clair doubted the Northwest Territory's capacity for self-government. The population, he wrote, consisted of a "multitude of indigent and ignorant people" who were "ill qualified to form a constitution and govern for themselves." He thought their remoteness from Washington made their loyalty to the U.S. government suspect. And Federalists feared, with good reason, that the first state to come out of the Territory would be a Republican one.

There was, of course, more to the General Assembly than political wrangling. The legislators passed tax laws, criminal laws, and a wide variety of other statutes. To encourage social and economic growth, they provided for the opening and maintenance of public highways, the costs of which would be paid for by a road tax, although anyone who did not pay taxes or who did not want to pay the road tax could work on the roads instead. In addition, men from twenty-one to fifty years of age were subject to a work levy of two days per year. The courts could also contract for the construction of bridges at county expense. The General Assembly passed various acts of commercial regulation or promotion. One statute authorized local courts to license ferries and to regulate the rates of ferriage. Another required every gristmill operator to keep a county-sealed set of measures and limited the miller's compensation to a specified fraction of each type of grain ground. Two acts passed by the second territorial assembly authorized private parties to construct bridges and fixed the tolls for crossing, and another provided for inspection of agricultural products being exported and for the labeling of the packages as to the quality and quantity of their contents.

To improve the government of the territory the legislature adopted an election law, revised the law providing for a territorial treasurer, and directed the governor to appoint a territorial auditor. In its second session the first territorial General Assembly created a municipal corporation. The act gave local voting rights to all adult male freeholders and taxpayers in the town, recognized the town meeting as the main source of political authority, and authorized the election of various local officials and the levying of local taxes. Other municipal incorporation acts followed. Before long, rural townships too received powers of self-government.

What the legislature could not do was create a decent transportation network. The lack of roads and the hazards of rivers hindered trade as well as government. Western settlers could not get their produce to distant markets or obtain goods made elsewhere. The obstacles to transportation made trade too costly. East-west commerce was virtually impossible. Farmers who could get their products to the Ohio River might be able to send them down the Ohio and the Mississippi to New Orleans, but that trip could be dangerous, especially at the falls near Louisville, and until 1803 a hostile Spanish government controlled the port. Besides, a round-trip from Cincinnati to New Orleans took six months. "The craft made use of were necessarily small," Jacob Burnet recalled, "and the cargoes proportionally light; and when they arrived at New Orleans in flat-boats, which could not be taken back, the boats were abandoned, and the hands returned by land, most generally on foot, through a wilderness inhabited by Indians, of seven or eight hundred miles." As a result, farmers had little incentive to grow more than they needed for their families and any newly arrived neighbors.

Without a transportation revolution—the construction of roads, bridges, canals, and eventually railroads—the Northwest Territory would remain poor and backward. It would take time for that revolution to occur. Decades after the eastern-most portion of the original Northwest Territory had become the State of Ohio, the people's elected representatives found the trip to and from the state capital an adventure. At the end of the legislative session of 1827, heavy rains turned the roads into impassable quagmires. To avoid being trapped in Columbus, two lawmakers canoed one hundred miles down the swollen Scioto River to Portsmouth and caught an Ohio River steamboat for the rest of the journey. In 1842 a legislator, noting the thick snow and ice, wrote, "when it does break up it will be awfully muddy and if the break up should take place about the time of our adjournment, it may take me a day longer to get home." Crossing streams could still be perilous. One representative had several unhappy crossing incidents in 1846. At one place his stagecoach traversed a bridge that was under high water. At another, "we found the plank afloat, and the driver and myself waded in and spent half an hour in the water loading the plank down with stones."

Even dry roads, with their dust and ruts, could make for hard traveling. One state representative, on arriving in Columbus, wrote to his wife, "I am here but in no very comfortable plight, I assure you. The roads were in such condition, that after remaining in Bainbridge until 10 am Tuesday morning, I have been bouncing on a stage every hour since." During his visit to America in 1842, Charles Dickens traveled by stagecoach from Cincinnati to Sandusky. The road to Columbus was macadamized—constructed in layers of crushed stone according to a method developed by Scottish engineer John MacAdam—but from Columbus north, the coach alternately jolted the passengers enough "to have dislocated all the bones in the human body" and threatened to leave them mired in mud.

British writer Harriet Martineau described the roads on her journey from Detroit westward across Michigan in June 1836.

Twice on the first leg of the trip something on her stagecoach broke, but she did not blame the driver. "Juggernaut's car," wrote Martineau, "would have been 'broke to bits' on such a road." On leaving Jonesville, she found the road "more deplorable than ever." When it became too dangerous for the coach, the passengers had to alight, but walking was no easier than riding. "Such hopping and jumping; such slipping and sliding; such looks of despair from the middle of a pond; such shifting of logs, and carrying of planks, and handing along the fallen trunks of trees!" Sometimes the road was simply impassable, so that the party had to detour through the woods, the carriage "twist[ing] and [winding] about to avoid blows against the noble beech-stems," the "waters of the swamp plash[ing] under our wheels, and the boughs crunch[ing] overhead."

It was no wonder that the governors of the Old Northwest pushed for internal improvements. With the return of peace after the War of 1812, Ohio's Thomas Worthington told the state's legislators that it was their "sacred duty" to develop the state's resources. "The navigable rivers and public roads as the means conveying the surplus produce of the country to market, are of the first importance to the state—notwithstanding the great fertility of our soil, if the surplus produced from it, beyond our own consumption, does not command a price sufficient to reward the husbandman, the spring to industry is in a great measure destroyed." Ohio had navigable rivers aplenty, Worthington declared, but they needed "artificial aid" to render them safe. "In the same proportion that facilities are given to the farmer to transport his surplus produce to market, are his profits increased. And without such facilities his labour is measurably sunk in the expense of transportation." Worthington's successor, Ethan A. Brown, insisted that "[i]f we would raise the character of our state by increasing industry, and our resources, it seems necessary to improve the internal communications; and open a cheaper way to market for the surplus produce of a large portion of our fertile country."

The other governors of the Old Northwest faced similar problems. "One can scarcely realize the condition of Indiana in 1825," wrote a Hoosier historian. "There was no railroad, no canal, no pike. All her rivers except the Ohio were obstructed by fallen trees, ripples, and bars. Two stage lines led to Indianapolis, one from Madison, the other from Centerville. The service was bad, roads frequently impassable, and stages usually late." As Governor Jonathan Jennings reminded the legislature, "The internal improvement of the State forms a subject of the most serious importance and deserves the greatest attention. It increases the value of the soil, leads to culture and refinement, induces immigration, broadens the horizon of the people, and prevents feuds and political broils."⁹

In frontier states that were perpetually short of capital, it seemed only logical that government should lend its assistance to the construction and improvement of a transportation network. Much of this assistance came in the form of corporate charters granted by state legislatures. We have already noted that America had a long tradition of aiding private enterprise in order to promote the public welfare, especially in the form of eminent domain rights granted to gristmill owners. Mills, though, were stationary. That was fine if all they did was grind grain grown by local farmers for local consumption. If farmers and millers wanted to reach a bigger market, they needed decent roads and waterways.

One way to encourage roadbuilding, or the construction of bridges or canals, was to grant charters of incorporation to groups of individuals who would, it was hoped, construct the needed improvements, in return for which they would be permitted to charge tolls. A corporation is an association of individuals that has an identity and a life of its own and that operates under a corporate charter. Before about 1850, every corporation received its charter by a special act of the legislature. In the late eighteenth and early nineteenth centuries, most corporations were cities, towns, churches, academies, libraries, or other nonbusiness organizations. The rare corporation that had a business purpose was usually a bank or a turnpike or canal company.

The legislature of the Northwest Territory never granted a corporate charter for business purposes. The General Assembly of the State of Ohio, the first state formed from the original Northwest

Territory, passed its first special acts incorporating businesses in 1807 (two banks) and 1809 (two turnpike companies). Only after the War of 1812 did state promotion of private enterprise pick up steam, as the Ohio legislature granted or extended numerous bank charters, authorized the construction of turnpikes and toll bridges, and encouraged the incorporation of manufacturing enterprises. In the meantime, the Indiana, Michigan, and Illinois territorial governments indulged in very little promotionalism. Indiana chartered a canal company in 1805 and two banks in 1814. Illinois chartered two businesses in 1817, just prior to statehood. Only Michigan caught the incorporation bug, but not until the 1820s, when the practice was spreading everywhere. Wisconsin did not become a separate territory until 1836, at the height of the internal improvements craze. Then the territorial legislature granted many charters for road, railroad, and canal companies. What none of the states or territories did was put substantial amounts of state money at risk by investing in these corporations or lending them money. Nor, with the exception of Ohio, did they embark on economic development projects on their own. The overindulgence in internal improvements would come in the 1830s.

"A New Map of the State of Wisconsin"

Published in Philadelphia, ca. 1852, by Thomas Cowperthwait & Co.

4

"A divorce between government and moneyed institutions": Wisconsin, 1846–48

Wisconsin, the last complete state carved out of the original Northwest Territory, was the first to hold a constitutional convention after the Panic of 1837. Neither the Panic nor public debt prompted the convention. Rather, after several abortive attempts, the residents of the Wisconsin Territory decided that the time had come to apply for statehood.

Wisconsin in 1846 was a rapidly growing territory. Between 1840 and 1846 the population grew from 30,000 to 155,000 and the economy began to diversify with mining, small-scale manufacturing, and shipping from small Lake Michigan ports. But agriculture dominated the economy, Milwaukee was the only city, and most of the territory remained uninhabited. The transportation network consisted of two military roads constructed by the federal government and a hodgepodge of locally built roads that were generally in poor condition. Even the original Military Road, the territory's east-west artery, was little more than a "crude and often impassable" lane.[10] The territory boasted no railroads or canals. The federal government erected lighthouses on Lake Michigan and provided some funding for harbor improvements, but not nearly enough to meet the needs of Wisconsin's ports. Attempts to create a territorially based board to supervise a systematic plan of internal improvements to be privately constructed failed in the legislature. Although Wisconsin's residents continued to plead for and demand more federal aid, appropriations ceased by 1845.

Wisconsin also suffered from a shortage of capital and of banking facilities. A number of federal actions—the destruction of the Second Bank of the United States, the transfer of federal deposits to selected state-chartered banks, sales of public lands, the distribution of surplus revenue to the states—together with irresponsible chartering of state banks and "wildcat" banking produced wild speculation in land. And a series of events, including federal actions and international economic developments, brought the speculative boom to a crashing halt in 1837. Wisconsin suffered from the boom and bust along with the rest of the country. The public blamed banks for the financial crisis and the depression that followed.

Wisconsin's first bank opened in 1835, when Wisconsin was still part of the Michigan Territory. The Wisconsin legislature chartered two more banks in 1836. Legal tender consisted of specie—gold and silver—which was in short supply in the West. But the banks had the authority to issue bank notes, which served as paper money. A note was supposed to be redeemable in specie; that is, a person who held a banknote could turn it in to the bank and receive gold or silver in exchange. That would rarely happen if people had confidence in the notes. Banks could give out their notes as loans and be repaid with interest. Borrowers would have a source of credit in the form of notes. And consumers and merchants would have a convenient form of cash. The system worked well, as long as banks did not recklessly issue more notes than they could possibly redeem, and as long as unexpected economic crises did not suddenly deprive them of specie.

Both of those unfortunate phenomena occurred in the spring of 1837, and Wisconsin's banks went bust. Mismanagement, fraud, and events beyond the banks' control led first to the inability of the banks to redeem their notes in specie and then to the closing of their doors. The people of Wisconsin were left holding worthless paper currency. Many reacted with revulsion toward the very idea of banks. The territorial legislature would charter no more banks. It did, however, incorporate the Wisconsin Marine & Fire Insurance Company. By accepting deposits and issuing certificates of deposit, the company essentially functioned as a bank. Its certificates circulated as the territory's paper money. Notwithstanding the soundness of the company's operations, its unauthorized banking activities became a major political issue in the 1840s.

The second Capitol of Wisconsin, the first in Madison; location of the constitutional convention of 1846–1847 (illustration from the American Encyclopedia, Columbus, 1859)

Disgruntled with the federal government over its inadequate support for internal improvements and its contribution to the financial crisis, Wisconsinites also found fault with the government's boundary policies. They believed that federal laws and treaties over the years had deprived them of land rightfully belonging to them. It was no wonder that by 1846 the people of Wisconsin thought they would be better off as a state than as a federal territory.

Wisconsin's residents had rejected prior attempts to call a constitutional convention, but by 1846 they were ready. The voters approved a convention by a margin of more than 5–1. As delegates they chose 103 Democrats, eighteen Whigs, and three independents, though the Democrats were a fragmented lot. Probably none of the delegates had been born in Wisconsin. Eighty-eight had immigrated from New England or New York, twenty from other states, and thirteen from foreign countries; the birthplaces of three are unknown.

Notwithstanding its Jacksonian political coloration and anti-bank sentiment, Wisconsin in 1846 was curious country for a radical constitutional convention. Democratic ideology had been trending in a radical direction since the Panic of 1837, but the causes of antigovernment feeling being voiced in New York and the states of the Old Northwest seemed to be absent. Except for its bad experience with banks, Wisconsin had not suffered the troubles endured elsewhere. It had no internal improvement fiascos, no huge public debt resulting from subsidies to railroad and canal corporations, no controversies over lopsided apportionment of the legislature. Territorial politics and a rising sympathy for statehood, not unhappiness with an existing constitution, lay behind the calls for a constitutional convention.

But antipathy toward government was in the air. The delegates to the Wisconsin convention had the baleful experiences of Illinois, Indiana, Michigan, and Ohio before them. Nearly 40% of the delegates came from New York, where a constitutional convention met in the summer of 1846 and adopted a radical document that Rufus King, editor of the Milwaukee *Sentinel* and a recent arrival from the Empire State, gave to several delegates as a model. Even Whigs advocated radical measures. One statement of Whig principles, adopted at a mass meeting of the party faithful in Madison in July, demanded, among other things, the popular election of all public officers; a prohibition against any law granting bank charters or "special exclusive rights and privileges"; a prohibition against the incurrence of debt by the legislature unless approved by a popular referendum; and a requirement that every bill of a general nature be read at least three times in one house of the legislature before being offered for passage at the next session. As a result, even without most of the major Tea Party issues, the Wisconsin convention of 1846 produced a Tea Party constitution.

The convention decided not to retain an official reporter of its proceedings, so there is no formal record of debates. In the early twentieth century, though, a Wisconsin historian compiled a record from newspaper reports, offering a pretty good idea of the subjects that occupied the delegates' attention. Among the most time-consuming were voting rights for blacks and aliens, the judiciary, capital punishment, debt collection, and banking. For the most part, these subjects did not involve Tea Party issues of the type with which we are concerned. There was some debate over whether judges should be appointed or elected, but most of the discussion of the judiciary involved the structure of the court system. Internal improvements received barely a mention. Only the banking debate revealed anything like the deep-seated distrust of government that would characterize conventions in the other states of the Old Northwest.

Wisconsin's Democrats divided into various factions with colorful names, but the chief division was between "hards" (those adamantly opposed to banks and the bank notes used as paper money) and "softs" (those who saw the utility of properly regulated banks and bank notes). We need not go into the intricacies of the banking debate here. For our purposes, the value of that discussion is what it reveals about the attitude of the delegates toward government. The convention's committee on banks and banking, chaired by Edward Ryan, reported as "hard" an article as could be imagined. The committee proposed to ban all banks of issue (that is, banks having the authority to issue notes) and to prohibit the legislature from authorizing or incorporating any institution "having any banking power or privilege whatever." Moreover, the report included harsh criminal penalties for anyone who issued notes or other paper intended to circulate as money or who otherwise engaged in banking-like activities.

The proposed criminal penalties led to a major rift among the delegates. Some members decried the permanent exclusion of banks from Wisconsin as shortsighted and the inclusion of penalties in the constitution as unprecedented and unwise. Criminal law was by nature a legislative matter; a constitution should not be complicated by criminal penalties, and the hand of future legislatures should not be tied in assessing them. One skeptic agreed with the "hards" that Wisconsin did not need banks at the moment but wondered who could say that the rapidly growing state would not need banks in the future.

Ryan defended the report. He insisted on the need to include the penalties in the constitution in order to restrain future legislatures. "Constitutions are made to restrict and restrain legislators," he declared. If you leave the question open, a "soft" legislature might come into power, and then bankers and "monopoly lobbyists" would besiege the lawmakers for privileges. Ryan likened the "softs" to the mythical, many-headed hydra, which sprouted two heads for each one lopped off. Another extreme "hard," professing his confidence in the people but not in legislatures, warned against the influence of money on legislators and demanded a "divorce between the government and all moneyed institutions."

When the severe penalties proposed by Ryan ran into trouble, another "hard," a self-proclaimed "fixed and inveterate" enemy of "the frauds and moneyed monopolies which . . . have plundered . . . millions from the honest and producing industry of the country," suggested an alternative. He urged that any person or corporation that issued notes or other paper intended to circulate as money, unless expressly authorized to do so by law, be subject to forfeiture of an amount equal to the amount of paper issued, as well as any other penalties provided by law.

Democrats generally agreed that the legislature should not have the power to enact special laws incorporating banks. One claimed that restraining the legislature from granting special bank charters was all the people had sent delegates to the convention to do on the subject of banking. But other Democrats insisted that attempts to make banking in Wisconsin virtually impossible contradicted sound Democratic doctrine. Wisconsin's growing population and commerce required flexibility to meet changing circumstance, argued George Reed. The people must be left free to act as they saw fit, without fear that they would "be untrue to the great principles and interests of democracy." In line with the laissez faire economic theory so popular among Democrats, Reed wanted commerce, including banking, to be left to regulate itself, except for such laws as might be necessary to prevent fraud and ensure equal rights.

Ultimately, the convention adopted a "hard" article on banks and banking. If it wasn't everything the most radical "hards" wanted, it came mighty close. The article prohibited all banks of issue and all legislation incorporating banks or authorizing anyone to possess any banking powers. It declared unlawful the conduct of any banking business, including the issuance of paper intended to circulate as money. The proposed constitution also prohibited any bank established by another state or by the United States from operating within Wisconsin. The banking article did not include specific penalties for violating the constitutional prohibitions, but it did direct the legislature to establish penalties at its first session. The banking article also outlawed the circulation within Wisconsin of any paper issued outside the state in denominations of less than $10 or, beginning in 1850, less than $20. The idea behind the prohibition of small bills, a staple of Democratic financial policy in many states since about 1835, was that the ban would force most people to use specie in their everyday transactions and thereby reduce the harm caused by unreliable and sometimes fraudulent paper.

Internal improvements and public debt generated virtually no debate. The committee on internal improvements reported a two-sentence article. It required the legislature to "encourage" internal improvements but prohibited it from incurring any state debt for the purpose without also providing a means to pay the interest and to liquidate the debt. The report of the committee on finance, taxation, and public debt proposed a state debt ceiling of $50,000, which could not be exceeded except as necessary to repel invasion or suppress insurrection or if the debt was for a single, identified project and was approved by the voters. The report also prohibited the state from giving or lending its credit to aid any individual, association, or corporation. To "lend credit" literally meant to act as a guarantor. Therefore, to say that the state could not lend its credit was not to say that it could not *give* money away in the form of a grant. But the delegates' intent was probably to bar any state assistance to private enterprise.

The constitution as adopted by the convention reflected the general thrust of these provisions, but it raised the debt ceiling to $100,000, and for specific projects it required passage by a two-thirds legislative majority rather than approval by a popular vote. The proposed constitution retained the notion that the state should "encourage" internal improvements, but only improvements by private individuals, associations, or corporations. And while it required the state to "devote . . . the avails" of land or other property granted to the state, presumably by the federal government, for specific internal improvement projects, it expressly prohibited the state from pledging its faith or credit or incurring any debt or liability for the projects. That meant the state could not promise to levy taxes or otherwise ensure that the debt would be paid.

The delegates adopted the one-subject rule for private and local bills and required that the subject of each such bill be expressed in the title.

That the chief executive officers of the state—the governor, lieutenant governor, secretary of state, auditor, treasurer, and attorney general—would be popularly elected seems never to have been in doubt. However, the delegates did debate the question of whether the people should also elect judges. As a federal territory, Wisconsin had had judges appointed by the president, with the advice and consent of the U.S. Senate. Most states also had appointive judiciaries. However, the trend toward popular election of public officials that characterized the Jacksonian era encompassed judges as well as executive officers. The trend began before the Panic of 1837, but the growing distrust of legislatures after the Panic accelerated it.

The convention's committee on the judiciary reported that the popular election of judges lay at the foundation of the whole proposed judicial system. In the United States, said the report, public officials must be responsible to the people, the source of all political power. The judiciary could not be an independent branch of government, equal to the legislature and executive, as long as it was chosen by either of those branches rather than by the people. The committee rebuffed the objection that judicial candidates for election would be political hacks as a slur on the intelligence of the voters, who would hardly imperil their own interests by choosing unqualified men for judicial office. Besides, governors and presidents had always appointed judges on a partisan basis; it was hardly a step backward to allow the election of judges who shared the political views of the voters. The report went on to address other objections before concluding with a hymn of praise to the "onward movement of the age" represented by the right of the voters "to elect their own judges."

Illustrating the difficulty of categorizing one delegate as "radical" and another as "conservative," Edward Ryan, an extreme antibank man, opposed the elective judiciary. Some delegates, said Ryan, seemed to think that "no Democrat can dissent openly from the elective system." But he pointed out that America was not "a pure democracy"; it was "a representative, constitutional" republic in which the people did not directly exercise any powers of government. The people wielded their political power by electing representatives to carry out their will. But the judgments of a court were not supposed to represent the will of the people. They were supposed to be the results of an interpretation and application of the law. Judges had to "stand on the eternal rock of right, unswayed by all the clamorous waves of opinion." The problem with the elective system was that the people would not choose the candidates; candidates would be selected by party caucuses, by politicians and not the people. It was one thing to elect legislators and executive officers who, whatever their faults, would always be looking back to their constituents with reelection in mind. For judges to decide cases on the basis of popular prejudice, though, would be to corrupt the judicial function. In an appointive system—and here Ryan was thinking of an appointment by the governor—there was "a terrible concentration of responsibility." A governor who nominated a "notoriously bad or incapable man" would never survive the outcry. For all the cogency of his arguments, on this issue Ryan failed to sway the majority of the delegates.

The convention wrapped up business on December 16, 1846, and sent its handiwork on to the voters, who soundly rejected it. Whigs, who were not as small a minority in the territory as might be supposed from their paltry representation at the convention, generally opposed ratification. So did a large number of Democrats. Much of the opposition stemmed from provisions that would have given property rights to married women and that protected homesteads from debt collectors. Under traditional Anglo-American common law, a woman's property became subject to her husband's control, and to his creditors' collection efforts, upon marriage. In the middle of the nineteenth century, states began to pass laws giving married women more control over their property. Wisconsin's proposed constitutional article aroused fierce opposition as a threat to the very institution of marriage and a harbinger of all the social ills that would follow from its destruction. Critics of the homestead exemption believed that it would discourage people from lending money to the poor. The homestead was usually a debtor's chief asset. Who would put his money at risk if he couldn't collect a judgment?

The third issue that stirred up opposition was banking. One newspaper accused "opposers" of "covertly" attacking the banking article by latching on to other issues because they knew they'd never succeed by openly basing their case on banking. Ryan, too, thought that the "real opposition," at least along the Lake Michigan shore with its commercial centers, was not to "married women and [homestead] exemption, but ... to the restrictions against banks, internal improvements, and state debt."[11] In fact, many Whigs and Democrats alike, fearing ruin to Wisconsin's economy, denounced the banking provisions. Even some who disliked banks and wanted to prohibit their incorporation in Wisconsin objected to the clauses that would prevent the paper of out-of-state banks from circulating in Wisconsin; they believed the prohibition to be impractical and impossible to enforce.

The defeat of the constitution did not mean the end of the Tea Party. In 1847 the legislature arranged for a second convention, which met in December of that year. With a smaller membership of mostly new delegates, one-third of them Whigs, the better-organized second convention went about its work with less partisan rancor. Its final document toned down the exemption provision (arguably, a provision antithetical to Tea Party principles in that it imperiled the property rights of creditors) and omitted married women's property rights altogether. The banking article was slightly less radical than in the proposed 1846 constitution. But the new constitution definitely bore a Tea Party stamp.

Recall the major Tea Party goals: fiscal responsibility and governmental accountability. In the area of state fiscal responsibility, Wisconsin's 1848 constitution set a state debt ceiling of $100,000 and required that taxes be enacted to defray state expenses. The legislature might exceed the ceiling in cases of invasion or insurrection or to meet extraordinary situations, but in such instances it would have to levy a tax for the payment of principle and interest. The animus against state involvement with internal improvements continued unabated. The constitution banned any debt for internal improvements. It prohibited the state from being a party to internal improvements, except to carry on particular works when it received land grants for those specific purposes. Nor could the state lend its credit to private individuals or business organizations. Moreover, the constitution directed the legislature to enact laws restricting the powers of cities and villages to levy taxes, contract debts, and lend their aid and credit.

The distaste for banking carried over into the 1848 constitution, which denied to the legislature any authority to create banks or to grant banking privileges. However, the delegates allowed the legislature to submit the question of "banks or no banks" to a popular referendum. With the voters' approval, the legislature would be able to grant bank charters or enact general banking laws. The constitution empowered the legislature to adopt general laws governing the formation of nonbanking corporations but prohibited special laws of incorporation except for municipal purposes or cases in which the object of incorporation could not be accomplished under a general law.

In addition to limiting the powers of the legislature, the second convention retained the requirement that every private or local law—that is, special legislation—deal with only one subject, which had to be expressed in the law's title. This requirement, designed to prevent lawmakers from sneaking favors past the public, would help ensure the accountability of public officials. For the same reason, the constitution made most major public offices elective, including the secretary of state, state treasurer, attorney general, judges, court clerks, sheriffs, coroners, registers of deeds, and district attorneys.

Wisconsin's voters ratified the constitution of 1848 by a vote of 16,759 to 6,384. In a place where residents lacked large-scale internal improvements but wanted them, where public debt from government-sponsored internal improvements was absent, where special laws of incorporation had not provoked major controversy, constitutional convention delegates drafted and the voters overwhelming approved a Tea Party constitution. There could be hardly be more persuasive evidence of the strength of the nineteenth-century Tea Party movement.

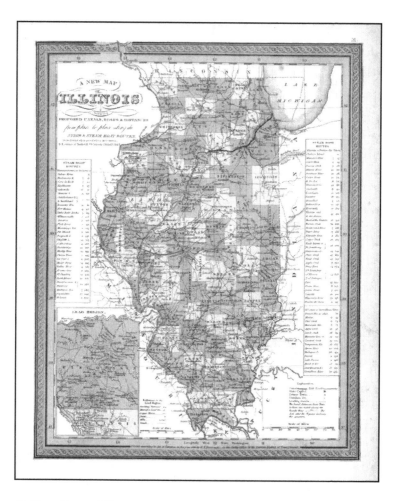

"A New Map of Illinois with its Proposed Canals, Roads, Distances from Place to Place, along the Stage & Steam Boat Routes . . ."

Published in Philadelphia, 1847, by mapmaker Samuel Augustus Mitchell

5

"To that branch we trace all our evils": Illinois, 1847

Unlike the denizens of Wisconsin, who adopted a new constitution without having endured a disastrous internal improvements fiasco, Illinoisans learned their lessons about government-sponsored economic development schemes the hard way. When Illinois joined the Union in 1818, thirty-five thousand people lived in the state. Almost all of them lived in the south, with the heaviest concentrations along the state's western and eastern boundaries formed by the Mississippi and Wabash rivers. Some of the area in between, and virtually all of the northern half of the state, remained a wilderness. Various Native American tribes occupied parts of the north, but the only whites seen there were fur traders. The prairie was tough land to break and farm; without some way of getting produce to market, few farmers saw any advantage in homesteading there. Rivers gave Illinoisans a way to dispose of their produce in New Orleans, but much of it piled up along with the produce of other western states and provided a poor return. Manufactured goods came mostly from the northeast, where they had to be paid for with sound money that western states lacked.

Better access to eastern markets and manufactures seemed imperative if the state were to develop economically. That meant internal improvements. The Erie Canal being built in New York promised to open the Great Lakes states to New York City. If only canals could connect the Illinois and Wabash rivers to Lake Michigan, the Illinois prairie would blossom with farms and towns, not just tall grass and wildflowers.

The Illinois constitution of 1818 presented no obstacles to state-financed internal improvements. The General Assembly reigned supreme, enjoying legislative power unchecked by explicit restrictions other than the bill of rights. The legislators also elected judges and most high-ranking executive officers. A council of

65

revision, consisting of the governor and the justices of the supreme court, had the job of reviewing all acts passed by the legislature and returning those of which it disapproved, but the lawmakers could override the council's decisions by a majority vote.

The General Assembly ventured into the internal improvements business in traditional fashion. It left the construction of local roads to local governments under general laws but passed special laws authorizing individuals to build toll roads or bridges. Sometimes the legislature appropriated money to help fund the construction of local public works. But the state had bigger dreams. In an address to the legislature in 1835, Governor Joseph Duncan rhapsodized:

> When we look abroad and see the extensive lines of inter-communication penetrating almost every section of our sister States—when we see the canal-boat and the locomotive bearing, with seeming triumph, the rich productions of the interior to the rivers, lakes and ocean, almost annihilating time, burthen and space, what patriot bosom does not beat high with a laudable ambition to give to Illinois her full share of those advantages which are adorning her sister States, and which a munificent Providence seems to invite by the wonderful adaptation of our whole country to such improvements.[12]

Economic development required not only decent transportation but also a stable currency. One historian described Illinois' currency in the early years of statehood as being "of an *opéra bouffe* character." Notes passed at forty different discounts, depending on the reputation of the banks that actually or purportedly issued them. "Some were issued by solvent banks, some by specie paying banks, some were issued by banks that had failed, some were counterfeit notes of existing banks and others of purely fictitious ones."[13] The delegates at the first state constitutional convention in 1818 so distrusted banks that they prohibited the creation of any new "banks or monied institutions" except for a state bank and its branches.

Illinois had four chartered banks as of 1818, but only two were functioning and one of those soon failed. The General Assembly established a state bank with the ability to issue lots of notes without adequate security. The bank made loans on generous terms with insufficient collateral, used its powers for political purposes, kept poor records, and turned out to be unconstitutional to boot. It fizzled out of existence over the course of a decade.

During that decade, Illinois enjoyed a population boom. Immigrants poured into the state, and the area of settlement spread northward. As elsewhere, sales of public lands fueled wild speculation. In the northeastern corner of the state, on Lake Michigan, the little port town of Chicago grew from two hundred inhabitants in 1833 to four thousand by 1840. All the new farmers, miners, and merchants demanded improvements in the transportation network. In the colorful words of one historian, "A state wide mania for improved transportation ended in logrollings and bargains which initiated a state system of internal improvements based on calculations imperial enough to have originated in the brain of Beriah Sellers himself."[14] (Sellers was the self-deluded visionary of Mark Twain and Charles Dudley Warner's 1873 novel *The Gilded Age*.)

The federal government helped launch the internal improvements extravaganza with a grant of land for a canal connecting the Illinois River to Lake Michigan. In 1823 the General Assembly created a five-man canal commission to lay out a route and estimate the cost of the canal. The law also directed the commissioners to communicate with the governors of Indiana and Ohio about improving the Wabash and Maumee rivers. After receiving an enthusiastic report from the commissioners, the legislature turned the project, including the land grants, over to a newly created private corporation, which, if all went as planned, would build a canal within ten years. The company would be allowed to charge tolls. After fifty years, the state would have the right to purchase the canal for cost plus interest. But the canal company soon gave up its charter without accomplishing anything. Illinois' lone congressman, Daniel P. Cook, wanted the state to own the canal and reap all the profits. In 1827 he helped secure another generous land grant from Congress, the last before Andrew Jackson decided that it was not the federal government's job to finance state internal improvements.

Over the next few years, the canal idea generated more talk than action. How much would the canal cost? To what extent should the taxpayers commit themselves to its financing? Should the canal be wide enough to accommodate steamboats? How much revenue would the canal produce? Would the state be better off owning the canal, incurring present debt in order to reap a future bonanza? Would a new-fangled railroad be a better idea? In 1836 the General Assembly authorized the governor to negotiate a loan of $500,000, with the full faith and credit of the state pledged for repayment. A new board of canal commissioners would sell public lands to finance construction. The future looked bright.

Unfortunately, internal improvements soon became tangled up with sectional jealousies over the location of the state capital, temporarily situated at Vandalia. Advocates of Springfield, including Abraham Lincoln, beat out the competition with a series of bargains, promising to support railroads and canals in various parts of the state in exchange for votes to move the capital to Springfield. And boosters of internal improvements in different parts of the state promised to support each other's schemes. No one worried about the cost of all these projects; huge profits from the canals and railroads would pay back the cost of construction many times over.

In 1836 the General Assembly chartered a host of railroad corporations in haphazard fashion. The charters varied so widely in their provisions that, had the roads all been constructed, "Illinois would have been covered with a railway system almost defying regulation."[15] The big fount of Illinois' future troubles, though, originated the next year with the enactment of a huge state system of internal improvements. Infected with the zeal of an internal improvements convention of leading citizens, which recommended a vast, state-sponsored system of railroad and river projects, the lawmakers authorized everything the convention recommended and more. All of it was to be paid for by borrowed money.

There were those who objected to this wildly optimistic plan. Representatives E. B. Webb and John McCown of White County formally protested the passage of the law. Illinois was already prosperous, they claimed. They found themselves "utterly at a loss" to see what benefit the citizens as a whole would gain "by plunging the State in a debt, the interest on which will amount to more than ten times its present revenue," which was already inadequate to meet the state's ordinary expenses. Surely some people would benefit from the increase in value of their land near railroad termini, but the mass of the people would be saddled with "burthens and anxieties." The act provided for the construction of many huge, disconnected works, the result of "what is in polite parlance termed compromise"—that is, logrolling. Webb and McCown denied that the successful internal improvement projects of Pennsylvania and New York furnished an example for Illinois. The public works in those states ran through "densely populated" country and connected existing cities of "vast wealth, business, and population." The Illinois system was designed "to *create* cities, and attract population and wealth." If it failed to do so, asked the protesters, "what will be the condition of this people?" To make matters worse, no one seemed inclined to finance the system through taxation. That would mean, inevitably, a dependence on banks. Given the sad history of state banks in Illinois and elsewhere, Webb and McCown foresaw "splendid failure and utter misery."[16]

But such skepticism swayed few lawmakers. The bill passed easily. The council of revision sent it back. Some of the council's objections were technical in nature, but at least one member believed that in a free government such works could be made "safely and economically" only by private citizens or corporations, possibly with state aid. The legislature made some adjustments to meet the technical objections and again passed the bill by comfortable margins in both houses.

Andrew Jackson's victory over the Second Bank of the United States in 1832 revived interest in a state bank to provide credit and a stable currency for Illinois. In 1835 the General Assembly created a bank that would be a public-private partnership. Under the original law and supplemental acts, branches soon sprouted all over the state. With the internal improvements excitement of 1837, the General Assembly increased the state's subscription of bank stock by $2 million, paid for by a state bond issue. At the same time, one of the state's original banks, the Bank of Illinois, which had been moribund for a decade, woke up and seemed to be doing well, inducing the legislators to subscribe to $1 million of that institution's stock, too. The banks were supposed to support internal improvements. The Panic of 1837 soon jeopardized both the banks and the improvements.

The internal improvements system would have disastrous consequences for Illinois, but it wasn't the only matter that roiled state politics in the late 1830s and early 1840s. Another one was the "life office" imbroglio. In 1838, when the Democratic governor sought to appoint a secretary of state, the long-time Whig incumbent refused to step down on the grounds that the constitution did not specify a term of office. The Whig senate backed him up by rejecting the governor's nominee, John A. McClernand, whereupon McClernand sued for the office. A divided state supreme court decided that the term of office lasted during good behavior or until the senate approved someone else. Democrats accused Whigs of favoring life tenure—not a popular position in a Jacksonian state.

Another judicial controversy involved the right of aliens to vote. Democrats, who generally benefited from the support of immigrants and favored alien suffrage, accused Whigs of concocting the case in order to get a favorable ruling before the 1840 elections. The trial court ruled that noncitizens could not vote, regardless of how long they had resided in their districts. While waiting for a supreme court decision on appeal, Democrats in the General Assembly launched a successful effort to reorganize the judiciary so as to reduce the Whig influence on the court. The new law embodied what twentieth-century Americans would call a court-packing plan, adding five justices to the existing four in order to create a Democratic majority. The supreme court put off a decision until after the elections but eventually reversed the lower court's decision. The brouhaha divided the Democratic Party and ensured that alien suffrage and the shape of the judiciary would occupy the attention of the public and the delegates to the constitutional convention.

As soon as the internal improvements law of 1837 took effect, the board of commissioners entered into contracts for the construction of more than a half-dozen railroads at once. The board got off to a bad start. "Not only were some of the commissioners guilty of at least neglect and mismanagement . . . but the enterprises were from the first befogged in the atmosphere of logrolling and bargain, under which the system had been initiated by the legislature."[17] When the nationwide financial panic cast doubt on the state's ability to pay for its public works and raised the specter of onerous taxation, opposition to the system of internal improvements began to spread. In 1840 the legislature brought work on the system to a halt. The question now was how to pay off huge debts incurred for a slew of incomplete projects. After the middle of 1841, Illinois defaulted on its bond interest payments.

In 1843, under the leadership of Governor Thomas Ford, the General Assembly enacted a program to pull the state out of its financial funk. The program included winding up the affairs of the State Bank and the Bank of Illinois, both of which had suspended specie payments in 1837 and finally failed; selling off all property the state had acquired in connection with the internal improvement system; levying taxes; and promising to pay off the state debt. The state also decided to complete the Illinois and Michigan Canal, for which the now-sober state was able to find investors by providing sounder security.

As early as December 1840, the General Assembly had before it a resolution to put the question of a constitutional convention on the ballot. The resolution passed in 1841, giving the people a chance to vote on holding a convention at the August 1842 general election. It's hard to say what issue carried the most weight in prompting the call. One newspaper listed seventeen reasons to hold a convention, which suggests a widespread disillusionment with government rather than one or two chief causes. Notwithstanding the financial crisis, dissatisfaction with the state courts may have overridden everything else, at least among the dominant

Democrats. Once the Democrats had reorganized the judiciary to their satisfaction, they lost their ardor, and voter apathy defeated the call. (A majority of those electors who bothered to cast ballots on the convention issue voted in favor, but the constitution required that a majority of those voting for state representatives approve the call. Many voters simply ignored the convention question.)

In December 1844 the lawmakers resolved once again, on a bipartisan basis, to put the convention question before the voters at the next general election. This time, the Democratic press pushed hard for a convention, and in 1846 the voters approved the call by a better than 3–1 margin. There were no doubt various reasons for the new-found enthusiasm for a convention, including a general distrust of government, but continued unhappiness with the judiciary seems to have been at the forefront. In the speeches made by pro-convention senators when the resolution came up for a vote, the subjects of internal improvements and state debt got barely a mention. The judiciary was uppermost in the senators' minds, followed by a desire to reduce the size of the house of representatives and fix the pay of legislators. Other issues included the need to establish the tenure of the secretary of state, prevent the division of counties for the benefit of speculators, and jettison the council of revision. One speaker hoped that a convention would eliminate the state's power to sell bonds.[18]

But whatever prompted the convention, once it met in 1847, the radical attack on government proceeded full-blast. An eminent Illinois historian, Arthur C. Cole, argued for the convention's relative conservatism. He noted that the Whigs, with the assistance of "bank Democrats," "had carried every point upon which they had cared to make a stand." It is true that the radicals did not get everything they wanted. For example, they failed to abolish banks altogether. It is also true that after the convention some radical Democrats expressed disgust with what the delegates had wrought. However, as Cole acknowledged, the Whigs often had to "yield to the democratic trend of the age."[19] That democratic spirit produced a constitution that no one could have foreseen a decade earlier.

The convention opened its proceedings on June 7, 1847, and wrapped up business in less than three months. Although delegates recalled with horror the "wild scheme of internal improvements," they spent very little time discussing either internal improvements or the public debt those improvements produced, other than how to pay the debt off. They simply took it for granted that the state should not be involved in internal improvements in the future and that the debt must be limited. The delegates instead aimed their ire at the institutions they believed responsible for the "wild scheme": the banks and the legislature.

A leading antibank delegate, Walter Bennett Scates, directly blamed banks for the internal improvements debacle. It was the banks' inflated currency and easy credit, he expostulated, that had led merchants into speculation and young men into extravagance—and the state as a whole, Scates seemed to imply, into the same sins. The agricultural state of Illinois, he declared, had no need of banks. Scates rejected the notion that banks could be useful institutions if properly regulated. He had often heard of well-regulated banks, he said, but had never actually known of one. Scates had a lot of company on this issue, and although the convention ultimately rejected a flat-out prohibition of banks, it made legal banking difficult in the state. It prohibited the creation of a state bank, barred the state from owning stock in a bank, and required that any law authorizing a company with banking powers be submitted to the voters for approval or disapproval at the next general election.

Banks were more than fomenters of financial disaster in the eyes of their opponents. They were, as Scates suggested, causes of corruption. The corruption extended beyond the temptation of individuals to distort the legislative process. Repeatedly, delegates linked banks with "monopolies" and "special privileges," as Democrats had been doing for years. "The system of banks heretofore, independent of all their other great evils," declaimed John M. Palmer, "is objectionable, because it confers upon them rights and privileges, not possessed by the people in common." The legislature might charter a corporation for a good purpose, argued William Bosbyshell, but who could tell where such favoritism might lead? "Next day the fatal precedent will plead. The door once open, ambition, selfishness, cupidity rush in, each widening the breach, and rendering access easier to its successor." Another delegate also warned against a proposal that might unlock the gate to special legislation. "Every year applications will be made, bribes offered, &c., by gentlemen with wealth, who may desire a private bank charter."

After much acrimonious debate, the convention decided upon the limitations on banking laws described above; the people would render the final judgment. As for other types of corporations, the convention settled on a general incorporation section that prohibited special acts of incorporation except for municipal purposes and "in cases where, in the judgment of the General Assembly, the objects of the corporation cannot be obtained under general laws." The latter clause opened a hole—unintentionally, to judge from the preamble to the resolution that introduced it at the convention—through which businessmen and their legislative allies would drive many times thereafter.

The assault on the legislature took many forms besides limitations on banking laws and special acts of incorporation. Distrust of the General Assembly ran wide and deep. One delegate traced "all our evils" to that branch of government. "If we had had no Legislature for the last twelve years," declared Zadoc Casey, "we would now be a happy and prosperous State." One way to contain legislative evils, of course, was to restrict the amount of debt the legislature could authorize. With relatively little discussion, the members imposed a debt ceiling of $50,000 "to meet casual deficits or failures in revenues." The provision allowed for two exceptions: (1) to defend the state from invasion or insurrection, or (2) if, at the next general election, a majority of all voters (not just those voting on the issue) approved the debt. And even if the voters approved, the General Assembly would have to levy a tax or provide another source of revenue sufficient to pay the interest, and the tax or revenue law also had to be submitted to the people. To further protect the people's purses, the convention, with no debate, prohibited the state from giving its credit "to, or in aid of, any individual, association, or corporation" and limited the

General Assembly's encouragement of internal improvements to the passage of general laws of incorporation for that purpose.

The legislature's penchant for authorizing debt hardly exhausted the delegates' complaints about that body. Their lack of confidence in the legislature stemmed from other causes as well. The General Assembly was too large and its sessions "were entirely used for log-rolling, &c., which took up a great deal of time, and therefore, the sessions were too long." The legislature had too much power to choose public officials and grant favors, with the result that people hung around the lobbies "consuming the time of members, and entangling them in schemes for individual benefit, to the detriment of the public interest." Illinoisans had been "cursed by too much legislation," much of it "unwise, hasty and improvident." The problem was especially acute at the end of a legislative session, when "bill after bill . . . have been passed into laws," with few members knowing what was in them.

The convention adopted a number of measures designed to curb the legislature. One, of course, was the limitation on special legislation, which the delegates hoped would not only stymie logrolling and favoritism but cut down the time spent on lawmaking. That, in turn, would shorten sessions and save money, since the members were paid on a per diem basis. To further discourage lengthy sessions, the delegates allowed the legislators the modest compensation of $2 per day for each day's attendance during the first six weeks of a session and just $1 per day thereafter. No bill making appropriations for the compensation of legislators or other officers of state government could address any other matter, and every private or local bill would have to deal with one subject only, which would have to be expressed in the bill's title. The size of the legislature was reduced. Fuel, stationery, and public printing would be let by contract to the lowest responsible bidder, and no member of the legislature would be allowed to have an interest in the contract.

The movement for popular election of public officials swept through the convention like a tornado. The proposed constitution provided for the election of the secretary of state, state auditor and treasurer, and all judges—all previously appointed by the General

Assembly or by the governor with the advice and consent of the senate—as well as circuit or county prosecutors and circuit court and supreme court clerks. The report of the select committee on the judiciary included a provision for the popular election of the attorney general, until then appointed by the governor, but the convention deleted it on the grounds that the proposed system of circuit attorneys made the office unnecessary. (The General Assembly reestablished the attorney general as an elective office in 1867.) Some delegates resisted the proposal to elect the secretary of state on the ground that the secretary was the governor's "confidential and constitutional adviser" and therefore should be appointed by the governor, but the suggestion that the governor appoint the secretary gained no traction.

The subject of judicial elections provoked considerably more controversy than the election of executive branch officials, as it did at all the midcentury constitutional conventions in the old Northwest, although the debate in Illinois still seems to have been fairly brief. Democratic lawyer Onslow Peters thought that popular election would destroy the independence of the judiciary, the great safeguard of the people's rights and liberties. Judges would be tempted to issue decisions with their effect on the voters in mind. Furthermore, the people were no more competent to choose judges than to choose professors of chemistry. Alfred Kitchell, another Democratic attorney, favored a split system: gubernatorial appointment of the supreme court judges and popular election of the circuit judges, who traveled around their circuits and were known to the local electorates.

Proponents of an elected judiciary denied that popular election would turn judges into "the mere tools of the politicians." That might be the case when a judge owed his office to one man, argued yet another Democratic lawyer, William R. Archer, but not when he was chosen by the people at large. Archer also insisted that the people were as well-qualified to choose the judges directly as to elect the governor who would appoint them. Whig attorney Archibald Williams observed that under the first constitution, judges were independent of the people but dependent on the governor and legislature, while the elective principle made judges dependent on the people but independent of the other branches of government. Williams clearly preferred the latter arrangement, but not because he thought the people so wise. Bad governors always appointed bad judges, he remarked, and the people had lately been in the habit of electing bad governors. No one defended the existing arrangement of having the General Assembly choose the judges. Popular election carried the day. Along with popular election, the convention abolished the life tenure of judges, cut the supreme court down to three members, and fixed judicial terms of office.

The ratification election was set for March 6, 1848, six months after the convention closed. Some Democrats thought the proposed constitution "too horribly *conservative*,"[20] but both major parties generally gave the document at least lukewarm support for being better than the 1818 constitution. In truth, although the new constitution reflected the numerous compromises made at the convention, it was a radical departure from the old one. The limitations on legislative power meant that an economic development program like the internal improvements system of the 1830s—perhaps the most significant public policy program of the state's first thirty years—could not be repeated. Unless the state was willing to impose taxes to pay for public works and the people approved both the works and the taxes, private enterprise would be responsible for future development. The legislature's capacity to bestow "special privileges" on influential constituents would be restricted. Office-holders in every branch of government would be directly responsible to the voters, giving a new scope and flavor to campaigns and elections.

The voters ratified the new constitution by a wide margin. They also approved a proposition, submitted separately from the constitution, for a property tax to help pay off the state debt, proving themselves more fiscally responsible than their legislators. All in all, the nineteenth-century Tea Party movement could claim a major victory in Illinois.

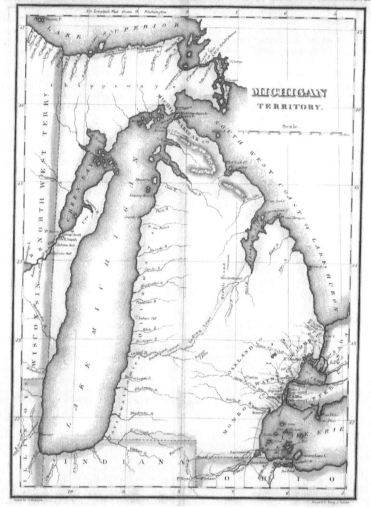

"Geographical, Statistical and Historical Map of Michigan Territory"

Published in Philadelphia, 1822, by mapmakers
Henry Charles Carey and Isaac Lea

6

"They forget they have a constituency": Michigan, 1850

Michigan entered the Union in 1837. Its first constitution reflected the values of Jacksonian Democracy at that time. All adult white male citizens had the right to vote. The voters chose state representatives every year and senators, the governor, and the lieutenant governor every other year. The governor, with the advice and consent of the senate, appointed supreme court judges, the secretary of state, the superintendent of public instruction, and county prosecutors. The legislature chose the state treasurer. The people elected the state auditor and attorney general, lower court judges, and county clerks, sheriffs, treasurers, coroners, registers of deeds, and surveyors.

There were few restrictions on legislative power. The bill of rights proclaimed that "No man or set of men are entitled to exclusive or separate privileges," but that didn't prevent the lawmakers from passing special acts of incorporation for turnpike, railroad, and other companies. The constitution directed the legislature to "encourage by all suitable means, the promotion of Intellectual, Scientific and Agricultural improvement." It also required the legislature to encourage internal improvements, the sooner the better. "[I]t shall be the duty of the legislature," read the constitution, "as soon as may be, to make provision by law for ascertaining the proper objects of improvement, in relation to roads, canals and navigable waters."

Unlike many other state constitutions, Michigan's fundamental law provided for two methods of constitutional amendment. One was through the convention process. The other was by a popular referendum on a proposal that had passed one legislature by a majority vote of each house and the next legislature by a two-thirds vote of each house. The second method was cumbersome, but less so than a convention; its successful use in the 1840s would help shape the debates of the convention that met in 1850.

Why the people of Michigan voted for a constitutional convention so soon after the adoption of their first constitution is not clear. One suggested explanation is that the public debt resulting from the state's internal improvements projects sparked a demand for constitutional restraints on spending. As we will see, a constitutional amendment adopted long before the convention rendered this issue moot. Another reason that has been offered is that the judicial system needed an overhaul. But in Michigan a convention was not necessary to modify the court system. In fact, the legislature enacted major judicial reforms during the 1840s. A history of the state attributes the voters' approval of a convention to "the ferment of Jacksonian democracy,"[21] and that may be as good an explanation as any.

In 1848 the Democratic *Detroit Free Press* thought there was not yet enough demand for a convention but that the people would insist on one in a few years. The paper was particularly exercised by the expense of long legislative sessions and the enactment of private laws. Should a convention be called, the *Free Press* promised to advocate the popular election of all officers; a limit to legislative sessions or a reduction of the lawmakers' daily pay; increased powers for county boards of supervisors; simplification of local government; and a prohibition of special acts of incorporation. The Whig *Ypsilanti Sentinel* questioned the *Free Press*'s sincerity, but the *Sentinel* observed that the Whigs for years had favored reduced pay for legislators, simplification of the laws, and the popular election of more public officials.

Neither paper mentioned judicial reform, internal improvements, or public debt as a reason to hold a convention. The chief impulses for a convention seem to have been the structure and administration of government: the perceived high cost of legislative sessions, the undemocratic nature of nonelective offices, and restrictions on local government. Reform in each case conformed to Jacksonian principles. In 1849 the legislature put the proposal for a convention on the ballot and the people overwhelmingly passed it. At the same time, the voters approved a constitutional

Michigan

amendment that provided for the popular election of judges, prosecuting attorneys, and all the major state executive officers. That took one big item off the convention's agenda. But when the delegates convened in 1850, they did not confine themselves to the cost of running the legislature or the improvement of local government. Instead, they used the opportunity to adopt a wide range of reforms.

Public subsidization of internal improvements would have been a natural target for the delegates if it had not already been addressed by a constitutional amendment. The heavily Democratic population of Michigan had pushed for publicly financed internal improvements in the 1830s. A booming territory with a rapidly growing population, Michigan in the 1830s had unbounded faith in the future. It also experienced wild speculation in land, based on easy credit. In this respect, Michigan resembled Maine, another northern state rich in white pine, water resources, and optimism, where "[b]uyers in the morning were sellers in the afternoon" and "the same lands were sold over and over again, until lands which had been bought originally for a few cents an acre, were sold for half as many dollars."[22] The speculative craze acquired the name "Michigan fever." To finance all this growth, the territorial and state legislatures chartered nearly twenty banking corporations. In 1837 the state legislature passed a general banking law under which dozens more banks organized. All these banks issued a flood of notes that circulated as paper money. In many cases, the notes had little besides public confidence to back them.

The legislature also fostered internal improvements. On January 24, 1837, the house committee on internal improvement submitted a lengthy report in favor of a vigorous internal improvements program. The committee had no romantic notions about the wilderness. Not so long ago, the committee recalled, Michigan had seemed doomed to "a perpetual desolation." Now, though, the state was on the move.

The sound of the falling forest is every where heard—abundant harvests usurp the rank luxuriance of her prairies—farms, villages and cities spring up on every side, under the magical hand of intelligent labor—the wide

81

embracing arms of her surrounding seas bear to her in-
dent shores a thousand keels, freighted with tribute to
the enterprize and industry of her numerous and enlightened population.

But if Michigan were to keep pace with the other states on the
"high road to national prosperity," it needed internal improvements. The question for Michigan, the committee believed, was
whether the state would seize the opportunity to develop the
railroads and canals that promised wealth or would, through
"timidity and apathy," let Michigan's neighbors siphon off the
treasures of trade. The committee had no doubt as to the "true
policy" of the state. Internal improvements, it declared, would
attract settlers, and that in turn would cause "agriculture, trade,
commerce and manufactures" to "rise up in natural and inevitable
order." The committee was not worried about the cost to the state
of building canals and railroads. The money spent must be viewed
not as expenditures but as investments. The committee recommended a state bond issue of $5 million to construct a system of
canals and railroads over five years. Taking into account repayment of the bonds with interest, it foresaw profits in the millions,
to be shared equally by the whole population and redounding to
the luster of the state. Carried away by visions of state-sponsored
glory, the house unanimously passed a bill in line with the committee's recommendation. The senate jumped on board, and on
March 20 the bill became law. It authorized the governor to
negotiate a loan of $5 million, backed by the full faith and credit of
the state, to finance the construction of three railroads and two
canals. The law also created a board of internal improvements to
oversee the project. At the same time, the legislature authorized
the state to subscribe to the stock of one private railroad company
and to loan money to another.

The legislative benevolence of March turned disastrous following the Panic of May, when banks across the country suspended
specie payments on their notes. By 1839 the hard times had hit
Michigan full-blast. Financial and other problems, including
gubernatorial mismanagement in handling the $5 million loan,

caused a rare anti-Democratic reaction among the voters. In November the Whigs, running on a platform of "retrenchment and reform," captured the governorship and both houses of the legislature. The legislature quickly passed an act blocking further state internal improvements contracts. Only a federal land grant in 1841, which allowed the state to pay contractors and laborers in "land scrip" instead of money, permitted some additional canal and railroad work.

The Whig electoral triumph was short-lived, but by 1842 it hardly mattered which party was in control. Most of the internal improvements projects stalled and would never be completed. The state had sold bonds for which it had never received payment, and even though the bonds had found their way into innocent hands, public figures spoke of repudiating them, which Michigan ultimately did in part. In February 1842 lawmakers adopted a joint resolution to amend the state constitution to impose limits on public debt. Under the proposed amendment, every law that would create a debt "on the credit of the state" by authorizing the state to borrow money or issue state stocks would have to specify the purpose—and only one purpose—for which the money would be spent. Every such law would then have to be put to a popular referendum at the next general election. The only exceptions would be laws to raise money to pay for the legislature's actual expenses, for the judicial and state officers, or for suppressing insurrection, repelling invasion, or defending the state in time of war. The voters ratified the amendment in 1843, giving the Tea Party in the Old Northwest its first constitutional victory.

In 1846 the state sold the only two internal improvements that had any value and got out of the internal improvements business. With state involvement in internal improvements over and constitutional restrictions on further engagement in place, the canal and railroad mania could hardly have been responsible in any direct sense for the people's approval of a constitutional convention in 1849. In fact, there would be virtually no discussion among the delegates of internal improvements or state aid to private enterprise. But there is no question that Michigan's experiment with state-sponsored internal improvements had left a bad taste in the taxpayers' mouths, a taste the delegates remembered when they convened in 1850.

Banks, of course, were a major subject of debate at the convention. Michigan's experience with banks was a bit different from the other states' but no less unsettling. By 1836 nineteen banks had been chartered by the territorial and state legislatures, yet with all the speculation and visions of glory, the demand for more banks and easier credit persisted. The heavily Democratic legislature, believing that special acts of incorporation benefited the few at the expense of the many, enacted a general banking law. Under this law, any twelve landowners who met statutory criteria, including a subscription of $50,000 of capital stock, could form a bank by filing papers with the county treasurer and clerk. Forty-nine banks quickly organized under the law. By various forms of fraud and subterfuge, many of these banks evaded the law and issued notes that would prove to be worthless when the land boom went bust.

At the convention, delegates railed against banks and heaped blame on the legislature for allowing banks to work their mischief. Robert McClelland, who had served three one-year terms in the Michigan House of Representatives between 1838 and 1843, asserted that legislators sometimes "forget they have a constituency"; due to "some unaccountable change" in them, bills that would not have received ten votes early in the session, when the legislators were "fresh from the people," later got enacted into law. Ephraim B. Danforth, arguing that the people should have a direct say in the enactment of banking laws, observed that it "is well known to every person who has ever been in the Legislature that the influence of the banks over the Legislature is irresistible." One delegate complained that proposed restrictions on the legislature's power over banking showed that the delegates lacked confidence in the legislature. He was right. Many members of the convention believed that legislatures simply could not be trusted. Some went even further. They did not want to allow banks even with the approval of the county or township electorate. Back in the 1830s, recalled one delegate, "[t]he people were as crazy as your Legislature, and would have voted for a bank, or a dozen of them, in every village or school district of the State."

Most delegates professed more confidence in the people than that, but the rampant distrust of the legislature ensured that the new constitution would include stringent restrictions to keep that body in check. With delegates insisting that they had been sent to the convention chiefly to rein in public spending and reduce taxation, it was no surprise that the convention imposed a state debt ceiling of $50,000, with the usual exception for the cost of fighting invaders or rebels. In stark contrast to the constitution of 1835, which *required* the legislature to "encourage" internal improvements, the new constitution barred the state from being "party to or interested in any work of internal improvement," except in applying grants of land or other property. The new constitution also prohibited the state from subscribing to the stock of any company and from granting the state's credit "to or in aid of any person, association, or corporation." There would be no more special acts granting corporate charters for private companies, and all banking laws would be subject to a popular referendum.

Besides circumscribing the subjects of legislation, the convention adopted numerous procedural provisions to keep the legislature honest. With longstanding complaints about the high cost of legislative sessions and "excessive legislation" in mind, and perhaps believing that the less often the legislature met the less harm it could do, the delegates limited the legislature to biennial rather than annual sessions. As an inducement to keep sessions short, they set the compensation of legislators at $3 per day for the first forty days of a session "and nothing thereafter." Each law could embrace only one subject, which had to be expressed in its title. The legislature could not amend a law simply by referring to its title; rather, to ensure that the changes in the law would be clear, the sections of the law being altered had to be reenacted and published in full.

The new constitution also required that each bill be read three times in each house before final passage. The three-readings rule was traditional. Its purpose was probably to ensure that the legislators knew what they would be voting on and voted after careful consideration. However, the rule did not necessarily mean that a bill would be read in full three times. By the late eighteenth or early nineteenth century, the clerk of the British Parliament read only the title of a bill and the first few words of the body. In the United States, state constitutions that required three readings usually allowed suspension of the rule by a vote of two-thirds or three-fourths of the members of the house in which a bill was pending. Suspension was supposed to apply only in cases of "urgency," but votes to suspend became routine, where the rule wasn't flat-out ignored. In some states, bills might be "read" three times, but one or more of the readings would be by title only.

Michigan's first constitution did not say anything about the reading of bills, but the joint rules adopted by the state senate and house of representatives required three readings on at least two different days. The new constitution said that every bill must be read three times before final passage. It did not explicitly say that the bill had to be read three times, or even once, in full. It is hard to know what the convention delegates intended, but given the widespread perception of legislative chicanery, they probably meant for every bill to be read three times in its entirety. The constitution did not even allow for exceptions in urgent cases.

One unusual provision of the new Michigan constitution addressed the late-session chaos that plagued many legislatures. At the Ohio constitutional convention, being held simultaneously with Michigan's, a delegate complained about the number of special acts passed at the same time, "with very little notice," at the tail end of a session. In an attempt to prevent last-minute log-rolling and legislation by inattention, not to mention stealth, the Michigan convention prohibited the introduction of new bills during the last three days of session without the unanimous consent of the chamber in which the bill originated. A few years after the convention, a legislative committee explained the provision as an effort to remedy the

> great evil . . . of hurried and dangerous legislation at the close of a legislative session, when nearly half of the bills of the session, and those the most important, were passed during its last four or five days, and many of them introduced within that period and passed without

being printed, and consequently without facilities for reading them or knowing just what they contained.

The trend toward popular election of public officials continued in full force. Michigan's first constitution provided for the election of lower-court judges but not supreme court judges, who were appointed by the governor with the advice and consent of the senate. Now all judges would be elected. Under the first constitution, the governor also appointed the secretary of state, treasurer, auditor, attorney general, superintendent of public instruction, and county prosecutors. Now all these officials, along with the state university's board of regents, would be chosen by the people.

The convention finished its work on August 15, 1850, less than two and half months after it convened. In November the voters ratified the new constitution by a vote of 36,169 to 9,436. The vote was another victory for the Tea Party movement of the mid-nineteenth century.

Excerpt from "Traveller's Map of Michigan, Illinois, Indiana & Ohio"

Published in New York, 1836, by mapmakers
Humphrey Phelps and Bela S. Squire

7

"Inscribe on the Constitution, 'No more state debt'": Indiana, 1850–51

In Indiana, the only way to amend the state constitution before 1850 was by a constitutional convention. Four times the voters had the opportunity to call a convention and four times they turned it down before convention proponents finally succeeded in 1849.

Indiana's first constitution, adopted in 1816, gave the General Assembly very broad powers. Indiana caught the internal improvements fever in the 1820s, and nothing in the constitution prevented the General Assembly from indulging it. Even before 1820, the legislature got the state involved in a couple of canal projects. Those endeavors failed, but at least they did not cost the state much financially and did not dampen public enthusiasm for internal improvements. In the wake of the great success of the Erie Canal, Hoosiers demanded the construction of a canal that would connect their state to Lake Erie (via the Maumee River) and to the Ohio River (via the Wabash) and thus to the world. Recognizing the horrid condition of Indiana's system of roads, the legislature also authorized the construction of numerous state roads.

After receiving a grant of federal land and negotiating cessions from Indian tribes, the state set out to build the Michigan Road and the Wabash and Erie Canal. Indiana's governor assured the legislature that these big projects would produce enough revenue to "relieve our fellow citizens from taxation." The road was to run from Lake Erie to the Ohio River. For years, the legislators fought like cats and dogs over the road's location before finally settling on a route. The proposed canal also caused controversy, because citizens from parts of the state not served by the canal did not want to pay for it, while railroad interests argued that state money would be better spent on railroads. After several years of wrangling, the General Assembly finally authorized the construction of the canal and the sale of bonds to pay for it.

In 1836 Indiana launched a massive internal improvements program with the passage of the Mammoth Internal Improvements Bill. The legislature appropriated $13 million "to crisscross the state with a maze of canals, highways, improved rivers and streams, and railroads."[23] Both Whigs and Democrats endorsed the program. But no one appreciated what the state was getting into. The state plunged into everything at once, with inadequate surveys, insufficient funding, no provision for the payment of interest on state bonds, and ineffective supervision over the expenditure of state funds. Borrowing skyrocketed; in 1838 the interest due on loans for the internal improvements system was nearly four-and-a-half times the state's tax revenue. Some legislators raised warning flags as early as January 1837, but the legislature failed to take effective action before the Panic of 1837 and ensuing depression broke the bank. In 1841 the Speaker of the Indiana House of Representatives mourned: "Here then is the end of our golden dreams. Here the consummation of all those visionary schemes . . . developed in the Wabash and Erie Canal, expanded in the system of 1836, and . . . terminated in bankruptcy, dishonor and disgrace."

It wasn't just the size of the financial disaster that upset people; it was also the way the legislators passed the whole internal improvements system. Advocates of "the System" in 1836 did considerable horse-trading to rustle up support for their grandiose design. As one delegate would put it at the constitutional convention in 1850, "It is a well known fact that that odious law [the Mammoth Scheme] was fixed upon the State of Indiana by a most infamous system of bargain and intrigue, of log-rolling and corruption." Among other things, the lawmakers agreed to grant a slew of railroad company charters in exchange for support for the canals. The legislature of 1835–36 passed nearly a dozen laws granting or amending railroad charters. The Mammoth Internal Improvements Bill itself directed the state Board of Internal Improvements to construct one railroad, to build another if a survey showed it to be "practicable," and to survey the route for a third. Railroad charters were, of course, a species of special legislation. As in other states, the legislature spent a lot of time on special laws incorporating businesses, seminaries, libraries, and other institutions, providing relief of one kind or another to private individuals, and granting divorces. After estimating that over six hundred bills had passed at the legislative session of 1847–48, one newspaper exclaimed, "In all this *mass* of *trash*, there were probably not a dozen [laws] to interest the whole people as a State."

The state debt and special legislation were not the only reasons for popular dissatisfaction with the legislature as midcentury approached. The lobbying and logrolling accompanying such major legislation as the Mammoth Internal Improvements Bill created an impression of impropriety, if not outright scandal, and the failures of "the System" tarred the legislature as inept. The General Assembly chose some of the most important public officers in the state: the secretary of state, auditor, treasurer, and presiding judges of the circuit court. Critics accused the General Assembly of corruption in appointing these officers. At a time when state legislatures elected United States senators, Governor James Whitcomb tried to trade nominations to the state supreme court, which the state senate had to confirm, for his election to the U.S. Senate.

Needless to say, Indianans had other complaints about their government. Popular suspicion of banks in general affected the Second State Bank, which was half-owned and closely regulated by the state. The bank functioned reasonably well under difficult circumstances, but it could not escape criticism during the hard times of the late 1830s and 1840s. Some Hoosiers complained that the court system was too fat and expensive, legal procedures too complex, and lawyers and judges too much given to twisting legal technicalities to their own purposes. Others wanted a better system of public education, closer regulation of banking and other corporations, or term limits for elected officials.

Democrats tended to favor the idea of a constitutional convention to remedy all the perceived problems. Whigs, usually the more conservative party, resisted the call until 1848 but then yielded to popular pressure. The Whigs set forth their demands for constitutional changes in a series of resolutions: direct election of all executive, legislative, and judicial officers; a prohibition on state borrowing, except in time of war, unless the people approved in a referendum; additional funding for the public schools from fines and forfeitures; biennial legislative sessions; a general incorporation law and restrictions on special legislation; a reduction in state expenses through a reduction in offices; development of the state's agricultural and mineral resources and "a fostering care of the mechanic arts"; and protection of homesteads from forced sale by creditors. It was a very Democratic-sounding agenda, and indeed the Democrats accused the Whigs of stealing their ideas.

The General Assembly placed the question of calling a convention before the voters in 1849. The voters responded with an overwhelmingly affirmative vote and by electing a nearly two-thirds Democratic majority of delegates.

The delegates convened in the statehouse on October 7, 1850. The main theme of the debates was the need for a simpler, less costly, more accountable government. Daniel Read, a professor at Indiana University and a fierce Jacksonian Democrat, set the tone in the first week by insisting that the state limit itself to the "simple duty of government" and not be "a banker, or a hotel keeper, or a builder of canals and other works of internal improvement." Although the executive and judicial branches of government and the state bill of rights received attention from the delegates, one member, as the convention approached its end, observed that nearly "the entire weight" of the convention had been "directed against the legislative department." And although he thought the convention had gone too far, he conceded that the people wanted such severe restraints on the legislature.

On October 26 the committee on state debt and public works presented its report to the convention. To keep the state from subsidizing private enterprise, the committee recommended that the state never be allowed to give or loan its credit "in aid of any person, association, or corporation." To keep state debt under control, the General Assembly's ability to borrow would be limited to a few stated purposes, such as meeting "casual deficits" or repelling invasion, and the debt would be capped at $100,000. If the legislature wished to borrow money for any other purpose, it would have to provide for a tax levy to pay the interest and then submit the whole plan to the voters for approval. The committee report also prohibited the General Assembly from raiding the sinking fund that had been established to pay down the debt.

Delegate Read made it clear that the committee wanted to separate the state from the private economy. Experience had shown beyond any doubt, he argued, that the government had no capacity to build canals, turnpikes, or railroads, to deal in stocks, or to be a banker. What have we seen over the last thirty years? asked Read. Hundreds of millions of dollars of debt heaped upon the states; public offices become "the mere foot-ball of contending political parties"; politicians pushing for local expenditures just to enhance their own power; "hosts of contractors, bankers, stock jobbers, brokers, corporation mongers, gamblers, speculators, and petty office holders, rioting upon the spoils of the State, and united to support the powers which most favored themselves." The only way to guard the state treasury from being plundered, Read insisted, was to get the state out of the internal improvement and banking businesses. Those endeavors were "most safely and economically accomplished by individual sagacity and enterprise."

Although Read cited statistics from both Indiana and Ohio to demonstrate the folly of state involvement in economic development, he made it clear that the committee's report rested on principle and not just practicality. Even if the state had made a profit from its loans and investments, it would still have been "utterly wrong," because "[m]oney making is not the business of the State." State monopolies were nothing more than robbery. A state partnership with some citizens to the exclusion of others was equally odious and more worthy of the England of Queen Elizabeth than of an American state.

Other delegates joined in the antigovernment chorus. Alexander F. Morrison called a proposition to prevent the state from being a joint owner or stockholder of any corporation or association one of the most important questions to be presented to the convention. The people of Indiana, he asserted, were still being "ground down" by taxes stemming from the system of internal improvements enacted in 1836—"better called a system of oppressions inflicted by the representatives of the people, as they call themselves, in the Legislature, by means of a regular system of log rolling." Corporations always had their agents at the legislature, Morrison claimed, and the people never knew what was going on until it was too late. The solution was to prevent the state, and the counties, too, from ever going into partnerships with profit-seeking enterprises.

The convention's antipathy toward debt creation was almost palpable. Whig delegate Schuyler Colfax, future vice president of the United States, demanded that the convention "inscribe plainly and positively on the Constitution, 'No more State Debt.'" The committee's recommendation that the state be permitted to borrow for any purpose if the people approved in a referendum sparked a great debate that did not set Democrats against Whigs but Democrats against Democrats. Opponents of the proposal feared that it would open the door once more to unlimited state debt. They worried about children having to pay for the improvidence of their fathers and about the majority robbing the minority via taxation. They insisted that prohibiting the people from authorizing debt was democratic because the people had a right to restrain themselves; indeed, restraint was the very point of a constitution.

State-financed economic development and state debt had their defenders, most notably Whig James Rariden. Men could not predict the future, Rariden observed. Who knew what contingencies might arise that would require the state to borrow money? Suppose a railroad company went broke. The state might be better off spending the money to save the road than losing vital rail connections. Public-private partnerships created internal improvements that stimulated markets. Without the internal improvements so ferociously bashed at the convention, Rariden maintained, the state would still be a wilderness. Over and over, Rariden and others who worried about hamstringing the state urged their fellow delegates to "trust the people," to let the elected representatives decide whether to borrow money or to subsidize private enterprise.

Given the hard and embarrassing experiences of the previous fifteen years, there was no chance that the arguments of Rariden and his allies would prevail. The convention ultimately agreed to strike out the $100,000 debt ceiling, but it prohibited the legislature from authorizing borrowing for any purpose except "to meet casual deficits in the revenue; to pay the interest on the State debt; to repel invasion, suppress insurrection, or, if hostilities be threatened, provide for the public defense." The new constitution prohibited the state from being a corporate shareholder and from giving or lending its credit. It allowed counties to subscribe to the stock of corporations on a pay-as-you-go basis but prohibited counties from lending their credit to corporations or borrowing money to buy stock in corporations, and it decreed that the legislature could never assume the debts of any local government or corporation.

Just about everyone agreed that the evils of excessive local and special legislation had to be curbed. The problem of local legislation—that is, legislation affecting just one county—was for the most part a practical issue. If the constitution did not provide that laws be general in nature, applicable to the whole state, argued Democrat John Pettit, then a man stepping over the boundary line separating one county from another would never know what the law was. Indiana would find itself with ninety-nine separate laws regulating the picking of cranberries. But if cranberries ripened at different times in different parts of the state, retorted another Democrat, why should there not be different laws? The members of the convention debated the need to delegate certain powers to local governments and whether the powers that some wanted to delegate were really just administrative and could be carried out under general laws passed by the General Assembly.

Special legislation for the benefit of individuals or corporations was different in nature. Unlike local laws, special legislation did not purport to recognize the peculiar conditions or customs of different parts of the state. Rather, it bestowed special privileges on particular people. "[O]n what principle," demanded Pettit, "can you say that you will grant to one set of men and not to another the right to construct a railroad or plank road? Upon what principle practically does it differ from allowing one man to set up a store or hat manufactory within ten feet of another?" Pettit was arguing against a proposal to allow the General Assembly to determine railroad routes. On the general proposition that special legislation was a bad thing, there was little disagreement. The constitution as adopted prohibited the General Assembly from passing special laws in a long list of cases ranging from granting divorces and changing names to supporting the common schools and regulating practice in the courts. In a separate article, the constitution barred the enactment of special laws creating corporations but allowed the General Assembly to provide for incorporation under general laws.

Local and special legislation had taken up a large and growing proportion of the General Assembly's time in the 1840s. If such laws were going to be prohibited, what need would there be for annual legislative sessions? The question cut both ways. With local legislation prohibited and the General Assembly "confined to its proper sphere," argued Othniel L. Clark, annual sessions would be shorter and less expensive. They would allow the legislature to continue as a sort of committee of supervision over state officers and would obviate the need for special sessions that would arise during the long intervals between biennial sessions. Beyond that, added Horace P. Biddle, annual sessions would keep the lawmakers closer to the people and to expressions of the popular will. On the other hand, if the General Assembly could not enact local and special legislation, which had taken up so much of its time, and if, as anticipated, the convention were going to transfer the election of many public officers from the General Assembly to the people, the legislature would not need to meet more than once every two years to take care of its business. Several members noted that popular sentiment overwhelmingly favored biennial or even triennial sessions. The convention reflected that sentiment by approving biennial sessions with a 124–5 vote. To ensure that even the biennial sessions would not cost too much, the convention limited the length of regular sessions to sixty days (later changed to sixty-one by the revision committee) and of special sessions called by the governor to forty days.

Indiana's Third Statehouse; constitutional convention was held in the Hall of Representatives in 1850–1851 (photograph ca. 1860, Indianapolis)

In addition to confining the legislators to their "proper sphere" and keeping down the amount of legislation, the convention sought to clean up the General Assembly's methods of passing laws. Nineteenth-century legislatures were notorious for logrolling. Because so much logrolling involved local and special legislation— you vote to incorporate my friends and I'll vote to incorporate yours—the downfall of such legislation by itself would have alleviated the problem. But there was still the possibility that even in general legislation lawmakers would cut deals for mutual support and roll their diverse pet ideas into a single bill. In that way, two bills that were each too weak to pass on their own would be combined and passed as one. Sometimes they would hide their arrangements by not revealing all the subjects of a bill in the bill's title. To make matters worse, legislatures usually passed a slew of laws in the final, chaotic days of a session. Laws would be hastily enacted by members who did not know what they were voting on. "Bills of the most important character," said one delegate, "were often passed in one day, and frequently in the course of five minutes, without having been once read through, or perhaps ten members knowing their purport." And in Indiana, passage did not require a majority of the members of a house, only a majority of the two-thirds necessary for a quorum. Because many members went home early, just over one-third of the members of each house—thirty-four out of one hundred representatives and seventeen out of fifty senators—could enact laws in a session's closing hours. The public might not even know who stayed and who left because the yeas and nays were not recorded in the legislative journals unless at least two members asked that it be done.

Convention delegates offered a number of measures to address these problems. One required a majority of all the members of each house to pass a bill. Alexander C. Stevenson implied that under the existing rules, "designing men" with "mischievous and sinister schemes" waited until members went home and then enacted laws contrary to the wishes of the majority. Requiring a true majority vote would induce members to stay at the capital until the legislature adjourned and would ensure that the will of the majority of the people, as represented in the legislature, governed. Some delegates disagreed, saying it made no sense for the constitution to allow two-thirds of the members be a quorum to conduct business and then require a majority of the whole house to pass laws. There might be times, they cautioned, when illness or other circumstances might force the absence of members; just a handful of missing legislators could prevent the passage of important measures. The harping on absences angered Christian C. Nave, who elicited applause by demanding that men elected to the legislature and paid for their services do their jobs. Lawyers seem to have been the chief culprits. "If they cannot afford to attend to the business of the people for the compensation of three dollars per day," declaimed Nave, "but must practice law in the supreme and district courts, why, then, let others attend to the people's business who are willing to do so." The clinching argument, though, was that democracy meant majority rule. Any bill that could not get a simple majority of all the members did not deserve to become law.

Stevenson was not satisfied with simply requiring passage by a majority of the members. To cut down on logrolling and to ensure that the members knew what they were voting on, he insisted that every bill be limited to one subject and that the subject be expressed in the bill's title. Objections about the difficulty of determining when different provisions were sufficiently related to constitute one subject did not faze the reformers. They could not countenance the common practice of stating that a bill had one named subject and "other purposes." The delegates offered examples from their experience. There was a bill whose "other purpose" was an appropriation from a fund other than the one named in the title. Another appropriations bill granted a divorce. Given the custom of reading bills by their titles only, the failure to indicate a bill's contents in its title was a serious matter. Indeed, the member who tried to sneak in the appropriation from an unnamed fund escaped expulsion from the house of representatives only because no quorum was present when the motion to expel him was made. The one-subject, clear-title rule would prevent such sneakiness and incidentally reinforce the ban on special legislation by keeping favors to corporations from being "slipped in" to general laws. "There are numerous instances," contended James Lockhart, "where laws have been stealthily repealed, or stealthily enacted, that could never have received the sanction of the Legislature, had this provision been in the Constitution."

On a related note, the convention adopted a section barring the amendment of an act "by mere reference to its title." Instead, the act or section amended had to be published "at full length." No one questioned the utility of the provision. And the convention required that every bill be read "by sections"—that is, in full, section by section—on three different days in each house. In an emergency the chamber could dispense with a full reading by a two-thirds vote, but not on final passage.

Most of these changes—the virtual prohibition of debt for internal improvements, restrictions on special legislation, the one-subject rule, and so on—related to the General Assembly's legislative functions. But the General Assembly did not just pass laws; it also elected the secretary of state, the state treasurer and auditor, and all the judges of all the courts. The antigovernment fervor sweeping across the state guaranteed that this power would be taken away from the lawmakers and placed with the people. The public sentiment on the subject was so strong that nobody challenged it at the convention.

The constitution went before the voters at the August 1851 state elections. Ratification was never in doubt. Both parties came out for adoption of the constitution, and every county but one voted for it. The great majority of the voters who cast ballots in the election voted on the issue, and eighty percent of them voted for ratification. The Tea Party in Indiana racked up a resounding victory.

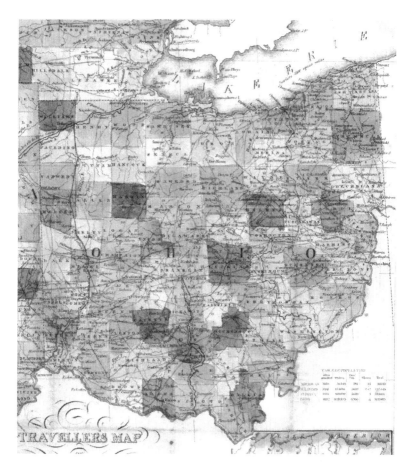

Excerpt from "Traveller's Map of Michigan, Illinois, Indiana & Ohio"

Published in New York, 1836, by mapmakers
Humphrey Phelps and Bela S. Squire

8

"The whole system must be dug up by the roots": Ohio, 1850–51

Wisconsin, the Old Northwest's newest state, held the first constitutional convention in the region during the period 1846–1851. Ohio, the Old Northwest's oldest state, held the convention that finished its business last. Ohio's initial constitutional convention had met back in 1802, as the territory prepared for statehood. The constitution adopted that year provided for no method of amendment other than by convention, and attempts to call a convention repeatedly failed. That meant that when the Buckeye State's second convention assembled in 1850, Ohio had one of the oldest unamended constitutions in the country.

Ohio's constitution of 1802 reflected the Northwest Territory's Jeffersonian political coloration. All white males who either paid taxes or worked on town or county roads could vote. Since the territorial laws already required all men aged eighteen to fifty-five to work two days on the public roads or to procure a substitute, the constitution effectively ensured universal white male suffrage. The General Assembly, the dominant branch of government, would meet for a new session every year. Legislators had short terms of office, one year for representatives and two for senators. Aside from the bill of rights, the constitution contained few restrictions on legislative authority. The General Assembly would appoint the secretary of state, the state treasurer and auditor, all the judges, and major generals and quartermasters of the militia. The constitution did not "encourage" internal improvements, as some later constitutions would, but it did not include any restraints on taxing and spending, either.

Skepticism about the General Assembly set in early and reached serious proportions by the 1820s. Leading Republicans, sounding much like their old Federalist nemesis Arthur St. Clair, described the members of the house of representatives as raw, ignorant, bullheaded schemers. During the frenzy of speculation and the banking crisis that followed the War of 1812, lawmakers, editors, and other concerned citizens fretted over the selfishness and dissipation sweeping the state and the rise of a "moneyed aristocracy." Federalists made political hay over evidence of corruption. They criticized pay raises that the Republican-controlled General Assembly and Congress gave themselves, denounced lawmakers who appointed themselves to other offices in defiance of the Ohio constitution, and decried abuses of the legislature's patronage power.

The banking crisis passed, but agitation against banks and other corporations—and with it denunciations of the General Assembly—reappeared with a vengeance in the 1830s. The storm grew out of the legislature's long-standing policy of encouraging certain types of business enterprise, originally with the purpose of establishing a foundation for community life in a frontier state. The policy accorded with the tradition of promoting the erection of milldams, turnpikes, and toll bridges. By 1815 promotionalism had picked up considerable steam. The General Assembly granted numerous bank charters during the speculative whirl following the War of 1812. The first postwar General Assembly authorized the construction of nine toll bridges and a milldam, granted or extended the corporate charters of a dozen banks in a single act, and incorporated the Cleveland Pier Company, the Kendal Aqueduct Company, and the Zanesville Canal and Manufacturing Company. The Zanesville charter authorized the company not just to operate a canal but also "to erect and establish water works, and carry on manufactures and banking associations." The next legislature, displaying a similar zeal for chartering corporations, continued in force indefinitely a general incorporation law for manufacturing companies that had been passed in 1812 and was due to expire in January 1817. Under this law, various types of manufacturing enterprises, and any powered by steam, could become corporations by filing articles of association in the county recorder's office and sending a certified copy to the secretary of state. The same General Assembly also enacted a general law for the regulation of turnpike companies. The turnpike statute endowed every turnpike company with the right to lay out a road and to take land, gravel, sand, or timber for the road upon payment of compensation to the property owner. Twelve turnpike companies received corporate charters during the session, most of them under the new law. The legislature soon created a procedure by which anyone who proposed to build a "water grist mill, or other manufactory propelled by water," could, in exchange for compensation determined by a jury, obtain the right to build dams that would cause flooding on lands belonging to other people.

In 1819 Governor Ethan Allen Brown called roads and canals the "veins and arteries to the body politic, that diffuse supplies, health, vigor and animation to the whole system." Over the next several years, canal enthusiasts in and out of the legislature pressed their cause. In 1825 the General Assembly authorized the state to borrow money for canal construction and to pledge its full faith and credit for repayment. Canal advocates muted opposition from some quarters by endorsing tax reform. They quelled resistance from districts that the projected canals bypassed by appropriating money for roads in those areas but not for counties on the canal routes. The Miami Canal opened in 1829, the Ohio Canal in 1833. Future governor Salmon P. Chase declared with satisfaction that Ohio's internal improvements had given the state "a name and character of which her sons may be justly proud."

In the next few years, however, the General Assembly expanded the internal improvements program beyond the state's capacity to pay. Everyone wanted a piece of the pie. With all parts of the state clamoring for internal improvements, the lawmakers authorized several major new canal projects. They also enacted the Loan Law, which *required* the state to give financial aid to private canal, turnpike, and railroad companies. Railroads, a promising new form of transportation, could qualify for loans of state credit amounting to one-third of their authorized capital if private investors supplied two-thirds of the money needed for construction and the state canal board foresaw a two percent annual return on investment. Turnpike and canal companies could receive state subscriptions to large portions of their capital stock when private investors had taken the rest. Passed at a time when state funds were already heavily committed to public works, the Loan Law set no limit on the state's potential investment in private corporations. It mandated state assistance even to poorly planned enterprises, and it invited fraud. To make matters worse, the state acquired its Loan Law obligations on the eve of the great panic and depression. Scattered skepticism about public works and public aid to private enterprise soon turned into widespread revulsion against state involvement in economic affairs. As early as 1825, some Ohioans had been anxious about the increasing state debt and the imposition of taxes to pay for the canals. Between 1825 and 1830, the debt increased nearly eleven fold, from $400,000 to $4,333,000. With the inauguration of new public works in 1836 and aid granted under the Loan Law, the debt almost doubled again and by 1840 exceeded $12 million. The Loan Law came to be called the Plunder Law. In 1840 the General Assembly repealed the law except as to certain projects that had already begun, and in 1842 it suspended aid under the exceptions. Skittish legislators backed away from further involvement in railroad and canal ventures, and a few radical Democrats even proposed repudiation of the state debt on the grounds that payment of the debt took money from the people's pockets and gave it to "the British lords and capitalists" who held canal bonds.

Unlike some other states that had embarked on big internal improvement projects, Ohio finished its public works program without defaulting on its bonds or repudiating its debt. Good fortune played a role; most canals were too close to completion to abandon, and operating canals were producing revenue. In addition, both Whigs and Democrats in the General Assembly resolved to maintain the public credit. The lawmakers pledged all the resources at the state's command—surplus funds distributed by the federal government in 1837, uncommitted canal lands, additional loans—to pay canal bonds. The canal fund commissioners used toll revenues to pay debts, and the state auditor, wielding authority granted by the 1825 canal law, raised canal taxes.

Having survived with honor the fiscal crisis brought on by huge canal projects and mixed public-private enterprise, the General Assembly had no stomach for future state-financed internal improvements. However, with the return of prosperity in the mid-1840s, the legislature readily authorized local governments to issue bonds for or subscribe to the stock of railroad and turnpike companies. Local governments plunged headlong into railroad schemes, many of which proved worthless. The harsh experiences of state and local governments in aiding private corporations contributed significantly to the movement for a constitutional convention that would limit the ability of government to incur debt and aid private enterprise.

Before 1846 calls for a constitutional convention, mostly motivated by the need to reform the judicial system or the desire to establish biennial legislative sessions, made little headway. But the combination of financial crises, bitter partisan conflicts over racial and sectional issues, the General Assembly's inability to deal with judicial backlogs, bribery and election scandals, clashes between the lawmakers and the press, and unseemly apportionment fights ratcheted up the demand. Between 1846 and 1848, resolutions in favor of a convention received majorities in one or both houses of the legislature but not the two-thirds required by the constitution. Proponents of a convention finally succeeded in 1849, when partisan passions had reached a fever pitch and popular disenchantment with government seemed deeper than ever.

In May 1849 Samuel Medary, publisher of the leading Democratic newspaper in the state, established the *New Constitution,* a weekly paper meant to whip up enthusiasm for a convention. Under the motto "power is always stealing from the many to the few," the *New Constitution* identified five key goals for a convention: sweeping reform of the judiciary, popular election of all public officers, limitations on the General Assembly's power to increase the state debt, an improved system of public schools, and authority in the people to "reform or annul" laws found to be injurious. By injurious legislation Medary probably meant special acts of incorporation and the "special privileges" they granted. In October the people overwhelmingly approved the call for a convention, and the state plunged into what one fearful Whig called "the wild sea of experiment."

The elected convention delegates met in 1850–51 to draw up a new fundamental law for the state. The document proposed by the convention did not shift power significantly from one branch of government to another, for the delegates as a whole were no more enamored of the executive or the courts than they were of the legislature. However, the new constitution did curtail the General Assembly's authority. "What kind of a General Assembly shall we have under the new Constitution?" asked a radical Democratic delegate early in the debates.

> [W]e must expect to have a General Assembly stripped of certain important powers which it before possessed; stripped of the power to enact special laws or creating special corporations; stripped of the appointing power; stripped of the apportionment power, and of the power of special legislation. We shall ... thus take away from them as much as possible all temptation to the abuse of their powers. All this will be done with special reference to the complaints that we have too much legislation, which have come up from all quarters.

In the minds of many, the legislature could no longer be trusted with the virtually unlimited power it had enjoyed under the 1802 constitution. One member of the convention declared his dismay at the evidence of "so much distrust of the legislative department." A stranger entering the convention hall, he said, "would suppose that we had lost all confidence in that department; and that we seem to be acting under the apprehension, that the entire body of our Senators and Representatives ... wanted to trample upon the rights of the people." In fact, most of the delegates *had* lost confidence in the legislature. The new constitution drafted by the convention and approved by the people imposed major new restrictions on the power of the General Assembly.

Believing that the world was "governed too much," the delegates decided upon biennial elections and biennial sessions of the

General Assembly (that is, sessions once every two years). Some delegates argued that the "safety of the republic" required frequent elections and annual meetings of the branch of government closest to the people. They maintained that the treasury needed constant watching and predicted that biennial legislatures would stay in session longer and then rush through legislation in their anxiety to adjourn. But proponents of biennial sessions remained unfazed. They noted that the General Assembly, convening annually, had not been very good at safeguarding the public treasury. They complained of the expense of annual sessions, the constant turmoil produced by annual elections, and the superabundance of legislation. The people, they said, were sick and tired of all the lawmaking, logrolling, and partisanship.

The 1850–51 convention heard many tirades against banks and other corporations and fulminations against special legislation that benefited particular groups of people. Most delegates recognized the utility of corporations; they complained chiefly about the evils of special legislation and debated at great length the merits of general laws of incorporation. Opponents of a general law pointed out two potential problems: the inability of one law to address the differing needs of communities throughout the state and the legislature's loss of control over individual corporate charters. Advocates of a general law believed that a statute could be fashioned to meet these objections. More importantly, they saw special legislation as the source of incredible waste and corruption. Three-fourths of the laws passed by the General Assembly were special acts of incorporation, they complained. Most of them were dead letters, passed but never put into operation. Logrolling legislators rushed special laws through in a mass at the end of the session after giving them little or no consideration.

Delegate G. Volney Dorsey expressed the prevailing view. Corporations brought together capital and labor in pursuit of enterprises "useful to the community," he said, "but the moment you allow your Legislature to grant special charters and to attach special privileges to individuals, then, all is wrong." Dorsey favored a general incorporation law not only to eliminate the nuisance of special laws but also "because it is more truly republican, to establish a general law, by which every association of individuals may be governed; for thereby you take away that corrupting influence always attendant upon the granting of special privileges by a Legislature, through which these 'special acts' are passed . . . by a system of 'log-rolling.'"

With a majority of delegates predisposed toward such views, the convention adopted constitutional provisions that prohibited special acts of incorporation, whether for business enterprises, municipalities, or nonprofit organizations; authorized the enactment of general incorporation laws; required taxation of the property of banks and other corporations to the same extent as individually owned property; and required a popular referendum on all acts that endowed associations with banking powers.

The debates over legislation conferring corporate powers inevitably involved the issue of state debt. Delegates angry over state subsidization of private companies that produced no public benefits and ran up huge public debts demanded that government "leave railroad, canal, turnpike and other corporate associations, to get along upon their own credit, without any connexion or partnership with the State whatever" and that "debt-contracting, loan laws, and money squandering may forever be put an end to— that the whole system may be dug up by the roots, and no single sprout ever permitted to shoot up again."

Not everyone agreed, of course. The report of the committee on finance and taxation originally permitted the state to contract debts for specific internal improvements projects with the approval of the voters. The committee chairman insisted that the report embodied the principles of Jefferson and Jackson. "Who shall say," he asked, "that the voice of the people shall not be heard?" But appeals to majority rule could not overcome the animosity felt toward the General Assembly for what many delegates perceived as the enactment of special legislation for the benefit of a privileged elite. By huge margins, the convention put into the constitution severe restrictions on the General Assembly's power to spend the people's money. It imposed a state debt ceiling of $750,000 and prohibited the state from contracting any debt for internal improvements. It barred the state from lending its credit to "any

individual[,] association or corporation whatever" and from becoming a joint owner or stockholder of "any company or association in this State or elsewhere, formed for any purpose whatever."
It prohibited the state from assuming the debts of any political
subdivision or corporation and forbade the General Assembly to
authorize any county, city, or township to become a joint owner or
stockholder of any company or to raise money for or loan its credit
to any company.

The new constitution restrained the General Assembly in other
ways, too. It required the General Assembly to tax all real and
personal property "by a uniform rule . . . according to its true value
in money" and placed restrictions on the creation and division of
counties, a major activity of the General Assembly in the past. It
banned retroactive laws. The constitution took away the legislature's power to select judicial and executive officers—the secretary,
auditor, and treasurer of state—and gave it to the electorate. It also
required the popular election of the attorney general, court clerks
and other local officials, and the members of the state board of
public works. Militia officers would be elected by those subject to
military duty. The new constitution included procedural safe-
guards against legislation by stealth. Every bill was to be read
"fully and distinctly" in each house on three different days, unless,
"in case of urgency," three-quarters of the members of the house
dispensed with the rule. No bill could contain more than one
subject, which had to be "clearly expressed" in the bill's title. An
act that amended a law had to contain the entire section of law
being amended.

The 1851 constitution did grant one new power to the legislature, although it was a power to propose and not dispose. The first
constitution could be amended only by a convention called for by
the voters upon the recommendation of two-thirds of the General
Assembly. The new constitution still contemplated amendment by
convention—indeed, it mandated that every twenty years the
electorate have an opportunity to call another convention—but it
also permitted amendment by resolution of the General Assembly,
subject to approval by the voters.

The convention was a long one, far longer than any of the others in the Old Northwest. The delegates first met in Columbus on May 6, 1850, adjourned on July 9 due fear that a cholera epidemic would reach the city, reconvened in Cincinnati on December 2, 1851, and finally adjourned for good on March 10. The voters ratified the new constitution on June 17, 1851.

The new constitution revealed the progress of the "American principle," as one delegate called it, "to gradually take more and more power from the government and leave more to the individual man." People simply did not trust the government as much as they had in the early days of the republic. Commenting on the convention's handiwork, Cincinnati lawyer Rutherford B. Hayes wrote, "Government no longer has its ancient importance. The people's progress, progress of every sort, no longer depends on government." That sentiment reflected the Tea Party's sweep through every convention in the Old Northwest.

9

The Tea Party Outside the Old Northwest, 1846–51

The Tea Party in the Old Northwest was a roaring success. For all the grumbling of radicals who did not get everything they wanted, and the assessment of historians that an alliance of conservative Democrats and Whigs thwarted the radicals' fondest hopes, the fact is that the conventions in Wisconsin, Illinois, Michigan, Indiana, and Ohio in the years 1846 to 1851 dramatically reshaped government in what was becoming the American heartland. Before the conventions, state legislatures had vast powers, generally unlimited except by a bill of rights and the threat of defeat at the polls. Legislatures emerged from the conventions with their powers drastically curtailed.

The Tea Party was not limited to the Old Northwest. From the Atlantic to the Pacific, constitutional conventions incorporated Tea Party principles into their fundamental law. Conventions in states and territories contiguous to the Old Northwest—Virginia (which still included West Virginia and thus bordered Ohio), Kentucky, and Iowa—all adopted such principles between 1846 and 1851. As we have seen, Iowa's two conventions, along with the New York convention of 1846, were precursors of the conventions in the Old Northwest. They portended the radical direction the conventions of the Old Northwest would take. Minnesota, which included a piece of the original Northwest Territory, conducted a convention in 1857. We will briefly consider the Minnesota convention in the next chapter. For now, let us look at the conventions in Kentucky in 1849 and Virginia in 1850 to see how the Tea Party extended well beyond the lands of the Old Northwest to encompass a vast, unbroken swath of the country.

Kentucky's constitution of 1799, the state's second, lasted for half a century, but not because the citizens loved it. The enormous patronage power of the governor and the county courts, corruption, a judicial crisis, legislative malapportionment, slavery, gerrymandering, and out-of-control public spending made a lot of Kentuckians unhappy with the constitution. In 1847 the General Assembly passed a bill to put the question of a constitutional convention before the voters. The voters approved the call in two successive general elections, as required by the existing constitution..

In public meetings and newspaper columns during the late 1840s, a general consensus emerged on the issues that the convention needed to address and even on many of the solutions. Broadly speaking, there were two major themes: popular election of public officials and legislative reform. The first was straightforward. To have thousands of officials at every level appointed by either the governor or the county courts was simply undemocratic. Perhaps if all those officials had done their jobs honestly and efficiently, the people would have put up with appointive system. But the wholesale selling of offices and other forms of corruption rendered the system intolerable. The matter of the legislature was more complicated because it involved so many sub-issues, but most of them aimed at one overarching goal: reducing the power of the General Assembly.

The 1799 constitution imposed few limits on the legislature's power. That enabled the lawmakers to dream of establishing a transportation network of roads and rivers that would open up commerce. Thanks to the state's abundance of streams, the citizens of Kentucky did not demand canals, except to get around the falls of the Ohio River at Louisville. What they wanted were good roads and improved waterways so they could move their agricultural products to markets and bring manufactured good to their villages and farms. After 1815 special legislation creating turnpike corporations—and later, railroad corporations—filled the statute books. "Soon state aid began to creep in as if by stealth and without system."[24]

By the end of 1837, Kentucky's investments in the stock of turnpike corporations exceeded $2.5 million. Towns and counties subscribed to tens of thousands more. The legislature passed a host of laws over the next decade extending its support to road, river, and railroad projects. The state spent a lot of money to make various rivers and streams navigable. The biggest improvement in water transportation, though, was the canal at Louisville. The canal company got federal assistance but no state aid. The canal turned out to be a great financial success. Cities and counties also got the internal improvement bug. They especially hankered after railroads and were thrilled to invest in railroad company stock. However, railroad construction did not really take off in Kentucky until the 1850s.

In 1844 the governor of Kentucky boasted about all that had been accomplished in the way of internal improvements. However, the state had "spent money lavishly on these improvements and often without proper evaluation of returns and general results." Carried away by the early enthusiasm for the projects, state officials underestimated costs and overestimated returns. The state debt rose accordingly. The Panic of 1837 and the hard times that followed caused the state to reconsider the whole notion of public support for internal improvements. The General Assembly finally decided it was time to wrap up projects then under contract and get out of the internal improvements business.

At the constitutional convention, which met in 1849, the first report of the committee on the legislative department included numerous provisions to reduce the power of the legislature and to make the lawmakers more accountable to the people: biennial sessions limited to sixty days unless two-thirds of each house voted for an extension; an apportionment formula to make legislative districts more nearly equal in population; a prohibition of "special laws for individual benefit" except by a two-thirds majority vote in each house; a ban on the giving or loaning of the state's credit, except by a two-thirds vote; a debt ceiling of $500,000; a requirement that every debt be accompanied by a tax to pay it and be submitted to the people for approval; the one-subject rule; and a requirement that every revised or amended law or section of law be re-enacted and published in its entirety.

When the convention came to consider the public debt, the animosity toward the legislature appeared in full force. One delegate claimed that most Kentuckians favored shackling the legislature to prevent a repeat of the "wild and extravagant use of the public money and public credit." He recalled how the proponents of internal improvements had predicted that all the loans would be repaid from the profits of the enterprises and how taxes would be reduced. But the people, "by sad experience," had learned otherwise and were saddled with a large debt and burdensome taxes. The people had sent delegates to the convention "to frame a constitution that will withhold such power from the legislature in future."

Of course, as in other states, the delegates were not of one mind on the subject of the debt, but the anti-debt delegates carried the day. A constitutional debt ceiling obviously indicated a lack of confidence in the legislature, observed one delegate, but it was the people themselves who had no confidence and who had sent delegates to the convention to impose restrictions. The convention adopted the $500,000 debt ceiling recommended by the committee.

No other restriction on the legislature stirred such controversy at the convention. The delegates adopted the aid-and-credit prohibition with little debate, in the process striking out the two-thirds clause and making the prohibition absolute. The committee's proposals to limit special legislation also sparked little debate. No one at the convention seems to have been concerned about special laws that granted corporate charters or economic rights. The delegates struck down the committee's proposal to require a two-third vote of each house to pass "special laws for individual benefit," but they generally agreed that the legislature wasted too much time on individual cases involving divorces, changes of name, and the sales of estates of minors. The courts were better suited to handle such matters, and the convention took them out of the hands of the legislature. The convention kept the three-readings rule of the 1799 constitution and added the one-subject rule with no discussion.

The committee on the legislature recommended biennial legislative sessions. Under the committee report, the General Assembly would meet once every two years. Each session would be limited to sixty days unless two thirds of each house voted to extend it. One reason for the limitation was the belief that government cost too much; another was that government did too much. Sixty days, most delegates thought, were more than enough to conduct legitimate legislative business. If there was one thing of which the people complained, insisted Squire Turner, it was "excessive legislation." John D. Taylor agreed. The people of Kentucky, he said, well knew that "the world is governed too much." Sixty-day biennial sessions, with a two-thirds vote required to extend them, found their way into the constitution.

The delegates also attacked the enormous patronage power of the governor and the county courts, with the result that most public offices were made elective. However, it was one thing for the people to elect sheriffs and clerks, another for them to elect judges. The convention delegates wrestled with the matter at length. Opponents of judicial elections predicted that candidates would be chosen by party "cabals and juntos . . . not for their virtue, intelligence or legal attainments, but because of their political popularity and availability." But portraits of the appointed judiciary as a noble body of honest and principled men above the political fray could not overcome public disgust with the patronage system. The "practical question," declared Silas Woodson, was whether the governor had "more discernment, more purity, more intelligence than one-half the voting population of Kentucky." With an eye on the "arrogant and sycophantic" men who constantly beset governors for office, the "lazy, idle, noisy partizans, who infest the country," Woodson insisted that the people could be trusted more than the governor to know who was most fit for judicial office. The convention went for the popular election of judges.

In May 1850 the voters of Kentucky ratified the constitution by a wide margin. Although the tea in Kentucky was a bit weaker than in the Old Northwest, it still appealed to the state's convention delegates and voters. The new constitution attempted to impose fiscal responsibility with a debt ceiling, a requirement that taxes be levied to pay for any obligations incurred, and a lending-of-credit ban. It sought to hold the General Assembly more accountable with the one-subject rule, biennial sessions, and a limit to the length of sessions. And it transferred the choice of judges and numerous other public officials from the governor and legislature to the people. Notwithstanding the impact of the slavery issue, which wormed its way into almost every topic of discussion at the convention, Kentucky generally followed the Tea Party direction of the Old Northwest.

Virginia was different, although even there Tea Party concerns helped shape a new constitution in 1850. The gross underrepresentation of Virginia's western counties in the state legislature counted more than anything else in producing the constitutional conventions of 1829–30 and 1850. Easterners had good reason to fear fair representation for western Virginians. The mountainous west cared far less for slavery and more for internal improvements than did the plantation society of the Tidewater and Piedmont regions, which dominated Virginia politics.

The constitution of 1830 threw the west a bone in the form of a slightly fairer apportionment of the legislature, which benefited the Shenandoah Valley but not the trans-Allegheny districts, but it remained a document out of touch with the democratizing tendencies of the age. It retained property qualifications for voting. It left the selection of all major state officials, including even the governor, to the General Assembly. Courts appointed their clerks, justices of the peace appointed constables, county courts nominated sheriffs to be commissioned by the governor. Judges of the higher courts held their appointments during "good behavior," meaning, in most cases, until they resigned or died.

Internal improvements and public debt played a smaller part in the movement for constitutional reform than they did in the Old Northwest or even Kentucky. Not that Virginia didn't have a debt problem. The state issued its first bonds in 1820 for the benefit of a private corporation. By 1831 the state had invested nearly $600,000 in private canal and turnpike companies, most of which operated in the east. The legislature continued to foster internal improvements, incorporating railroad and canal companies and authorizing them to borrow on the state's credit. The state also borrowed money to invest in railroad corporations. The state debt exceeded $1 million by 1833 and $3.5 million by 1837.

Unlike every other state we have looked at so far, Virginia did not suffer greatly from the Panic of 1837. The state had "an excellent and conservative system of banks from the beginning"[25] and no huge tracts of federal land to dispose of, so the wildcat banking and speculative craze that afflicted other states bypassed Virginia. Moreover, the demand for internal improvements had not been sated. The inhabitants of Norfolk, an Atlantic port with great commercial ambitions but no rail service, wanted a railroad connection to the west. The western counties, in turn, wanted their share of state assistance to link them with eastern markets. Travel between the eastern and western parts of the state remained difficult. A. H. H. Stuart, elected to the state legislature from Staunton in 1836, described an arduous, expensive, three-day journey to Richmond to take his seat.

> I left my home in Staunton in the stage, at two o'clock in the morning, and after a laborious day's travel, walking up the mountains at Rockfish Gap, and, after we got into the red lands of Albemarle, occasionally assisting in prizing the coach out of the mud with fence rails, we arrived at Charlottesville at two o'clock in the morning, and after a laborious journey of fifteen hours, arrived at Wilmington in Fluvanna. The third day we left Wilmington at twelve o'clock at night, and arrived at Richmond an hour or two after dark. According to my best recollection, the stage fare was $11 or $12, and the cost of eight meals and two nights' lodgings, at 50 cents each, was $5, making the aggregate cost of the trip $16 or $17.[26]

Not surprisingly, Stuart became a great advocate of internal improvements. State funding of internal improvements continued to rise, and along with it the state debt, which at the beginning of 1839 stood at more than $5.6 million. The growth continued unchecked right up to the Civil War.

So what happened at the 1850 constitutional convention? The west's "eternal clamour for the purse strings" alarmed eastern delegates, who worried that legislative apportionment based solely on population would allow westerners to tax eastern slave property to finance western internal improvements.[27] The east protected its property interest by writing favorable tax provisions into the constitution, not by restraining the state from engaging in the internal improvements business. The new constitution included no debt ceiling and no direct prohibition of state-financed internal improvements.

Still, the rising state debt and the experiences of other states caused convention delegates anxiety over the General Assembly's "power of mortgaging, *ad libertum* the property and labor of the people of this State."[28] The convention addressed the problem by prohibiting the state from pledging its credit for the payment of any corporate debt and from issuing bonds that did not mature within thirty-four years. It also created a sinking fund for the payment of state debts and authorized the state to sell any corporate stock it owned, provided the proceeds went into the sinking fund. Furthermore, any bill that levied a tax or created a state debt would have to be passed by a majority of all the members elected to each house of the legislature, not just by a majority of the members who happened to be present at the time of the vote.

By themselves, and by the Tea Party standards of the day, these reforms were tepid, but in other respects the new constitution reflected the populist constitutionalism of 1850. The constitution abolished the last vestiges of property qualifications for voting. It included the by-now familiar one-subject rule and the rule requiring that any law revived or amended by a new act be printed in full and not simply referred to by its title. To increase transparency even further, the constitution required that whenever the legislators voted on a bill that levied a tax or created a state debt, the names of those voting for and against the bill be recorded in the legislative journals. And to limit legislative mischief more generally, sessions would be biennial rather than annual and would be limited to ninety days unless extended for a single, thirty-day period by a three-fifths majority vote in each house.

Finally, the popular insistence on accountability of public officials caused the convention to make most key public offices elective. The secretary of state, state treasurer, and state auditor would be chosen by the General Assembly, but the governor, lieutenant governor, attorney general, and all judges would be elected by the people. The voters would also elect the Board of Public Works, court clerks, prosecuting attorneys, county surveyors, sheriffs, constables, commissioners of revenue, and overseers of the poor.

In a state that had not suffered catastrophically from the Panic of 1837 and in which the chief grievance of constitutional reformers was malapportionment of the legislature, Virginia's 1850 convention turned out to be remarkably in tune with the Tea Party sentiments of the Old Northwest. This consistency is even more notable when one considers that the generally conservative east controlled the convention. This was because slaves were counted in the apportionment of delegates, and most slaves lived in the east. At the ratification election in October 1850, both east and west approved the constitution by a combined 7–1 margin.

California, Maryland, New Hampshire, and Vermont also held constitutional conventions in 1849–50. Under Vermont's peculiar system of constitutional revision, the people elected a council of censors every seven years to review the constitution, recommend any amendments it thought necessary, and call a convention to consider proposed amendments. A convention had no power to go beyond the council's suggestions. In 1848 the council recommended that certain local officials appointed by the state legislature instead be elected by the voters. A convention met in 1850 and adopted the proposal.

New Hampshire was constitutionally conservative, making just one change in its constitution between 1792 and 1877. The constitution required that the question of calling a convention be put on the ballot every seven years, but the people routinely voted no. A convention finally met in 1850 and put a number of Tea-Party-type proposals on the ballot, but the voters rejected all of them. New Hampshire thus bucked the trend of the times. In Maryland, on the other hand, outdated legislative apportionment and an internal improvements disaster led to popular demands for a convention and the ratification of a new constitution in 1851. The new constitution provided for fairer legislative apportionment and included the whole panoply of Tea Party reforms.

Nothing better illustrates the power of Tea Party ideology in the middle of the nineteenth century than the California constitution. The United States gained possession of California as a result of the Mexican War, which ended in 1848. The Gold Rush of 1849 brought tens of thousands of fortune seekers, making the organization of government a necessity. A constitutional convention met that year. With no local history to build on—no internal improvements craze, no skyrocketing public debt, no legislative logrolling for the benefit of corporations, no unaccountable government—the delegates swam with the tide from east of the Mississippi. They guaranteed universal white male suffrage and made the governor, lieutenant governor, judges, court clerks, and county officers electable by the people. They imposed a debt ceiling, which could be exceeded only by a law specifying the purpose of the debt, providing a means for its payment, and approved by a popular referendum. The new constitution prohibited special acts of incorporation, forbade banks from issuing notes that might serve as paper currency, and imposed personal liability on shareholders for corporate debts. It prohibited the state from giving or lending its aid or credit to private enterprises and barred the state from owning corporate stock. The constitution also included the one-subject rule and required that taxation be by a uniform rule and according to value. About the only nonradical feature of the new constitution was the appointment of major executive-branch officers by the governor or legislature. Clearly, the Chinese tea brought to California by clipper ships in the wake of the Gold Rush wasn't the only type of tea for which Californians thirsted in 1850.

10

Epilogue

By the time the Territory of Minnesota held a constitutional convention in the summer of 1857, the Jacksonian Era was over and the nature of the nation's politics had changed. The antiliquor crusade of the late 1840s and early 1850s disrupted traditional party alignments. Then the Kansas-Nebraska Act of 1854, which threatened to open the western territories to slavery, destroyed the Whig Party altogether and led to the rise of the Republicans. Although another financial crisis, the Panic of 1857, hit while the Minnesota convention was in session, questions of banking, internal improvements, public debt, and the popular election of public officials no longer dominated state-level constitutional thought the way they had just seven or eight years earlier.

On the other hand, such ideas had become so commonplace by 1857 that they found their way into the Minnesota constitution with little controversy. The constitution provided for the popular election of judges, the secretary of state and other important members of the executive branch, and county and township officials. It included several requirements to enhance the integrity of legislation procedure: that every bill be read "at length" at least twice in each house, that every bill deal with just one subject expressed in the title, and that no bill be passed on the day of adjournment. The constitution prohibited the creation of corporations by special laws and barred the state from giving or loaning its credit or engaging in internal improvements (except to the extent that land had been granted to the state for that purpose). To ensure fiscal responsibility, the legislature would have to impose taxes sufficient to meet the state's estimated expenses for each year. For extraordinary expenses, the legislature could, by a two-thirds vote in each house, create debt not exceeding $250,000, but the lawmakers would have to impose sufficient taxes to pay the annual interest and to retire the debt within ten years.

Although Tea Party sentiments clearly shaped the Minnesota constitution, the tug-of-war between distrust of government and dreams of government-sponsored prosperity caused a spectacular flip-flop in the next few years. Minnesotans quickly came to regret the lending-of-credit prohibition. They wanted railroads, and Congress had granted the state a lot of land for the purpose. But the four railroad companies that had acquired rights to the railroad lands from the territorial legislature needed a stimulus following the Panic of 1857. Even before the constitution took effect, the railroads and their friends in government proposed an amendment authorizing a loan of the state's credit of $5 million to be divvied up equally among the four companies. "Positive assurances were given the voters by all parties concerned . . . that this was not a loan of state money but merely one of credit, and that the taxpayers of Minnesota could never in any possible contingency be called upon to pay any tax for the repayment of this loan."[29] The amendment passed and bonds totaling $2,275,000 were issued. But the scheme turned sour so fast that the voters drove out the party in power (the Democrats) in 1859 and once again amended the constitution to undo the mischief. The new amendment "expunged" the first one and prohibited any further issuance of state railroad bonds.

Minnesota's experience puts on display the ambivalence of the American mind toward state sponsorship of economic development. The Tea Party revolution of the mid-nineteenth century had lasting effects. Through all the upheavals of the rest of the century—Civil War, Reconstruction, industrial revolution, massive immigration, urbanization—the Tea Party reforms persisted. Every state admitted to the Union between 1851 and 1900—all fourteen of them, from West Virginia to Washington—adopted a Tea Party constitution. They varied in detail, but most of them were strikingly similar. On the other hand, demands for governmental action, whether promotional in nature or regulatory (as it more and more became with the rise of big business, big labor, big cities, big

Epilogue

everything), challenged the very premises that underlay some of the major constitutional reforms of the years around 1850.

It is not the purpose of this book to trace the history of popular movements or constitutional development beyond those years, but to end the story of the midcentury Tea Party movement in the 1850s would leave a false impression of unbroken success. To get a glimpse of how the Tea Party revolution fared after that point, let's look at the late-nineteenth-century constitution of North Dakota.

North Dakota joined the Union in 1889. The state was a long way, in time, space, and condition, from the New York of 1846 and the Ohio of 1850; yet its constitution reflected the same concerns that inspired the midcentury constitutions. It limited regular sessions of the legislature to sixty days every other year. It included the single-subject rule, required the publication "at length" of any "bill" that was amended, and also required that the first and third readings of a bill be "at length" and not merely by title. The constitution barred the enactment of special or local laws in thirty-five specified areas and also barred special legislation in any other case in which a general law could be made applicable. In a separate section, the constitution prohibited special laws granting or amending the charters of business corporations. It included state and local debt ceilings and a requirement that taxes be levied to ensure that any debts would be paid. The constitution prevented the state and political subdivisions from lending their credit or subscribing to the stock of any corporation, and it prohibited the state from engaging in any work of internal improvement unless authorized by a two-thirds vote of the people. And of course the constitution made all key public offices—including the commissioners of railroads, insurance, and agriculture and labor—elective.

In short, long after the Tea Party revolution of the mid-nineteenth century, its principles were still being embodied in state constitutions as a matter of course. But by 1889, change was in the air. Hostility toward state legislatures had hardly abated since 1850. If anything, the reputation of the legislatures had sunk even lower, thanks to rampant corruption and an inability to deal with the problems of a rapidly changing society. One congressman complained, "This country is fast becoming filled with gigantic corporations wielding and controlling immense aggregations of money and thereby commanding great influence and power. It is notorious in many State Legislatures that these influences are often controlling, so that in effect they become the ruling power of the State." The foundations of the Progressive Era were being laid.

One of the most significant items in the North Dakota constitution was the section providing for the popular election of commissioners of railroads, insurance, and agriculture and labor. North Dakota entered upon statehood with regulatory goals. State officials with investigatory and limited regulatory powers existed in the older states before 1889, but the rise of powerful corporations, especially railroads, after the Civil War stirred up anticorporate animosities not unlike those the Jacksonian Democrats of yore had held toward banks. But many Jacksonians had wanted to destroy banks, not regulate them. North Dakota could not do without railroads. Great railroad corporations had largely created the state. North Dakota was not a stronghold of Populism or Progressivism—political movements of the late nineteenth and early twentieth centuries that urged greater regulation of business by government—yet the drafters of the constitution took it for granted that the state would be in the business of regulating business.

Some historians contend that calls for government regulation in the late nineteenth century grew logically out of Jacksonian thought. They argue that antebellum Jacksonian Democrats sought limited government because, in their day, government was *abetting* the concentration of power in the hands of a wealthy elite. After the Civil War, though, government could be used to *counter* the concentration of power in big business that was taking place without the aid of government. That the latter-day turn toward government, for whatever reason, represented the essence of Jacksonian Democracy is debatable. One wonders what Jacksonians of 1850 who insisted that "the world is governed too much" and who imposed severe limits on the powers of legislatures would have thought of the proliferation of regulatory agencies during the Progressive Era.

Be that as it may, the Tea Party strictures written into the new constitutions of the mid-nineteenth century did not prevent evasion and backsliding. Some courts held the procedural innovations of the midcentury constitutions to be "directory" in nature; that is, that constitutional rules for the legislative process, such as the single-subject and clear-title rules, were meant as requirements *for* the legislature, to be enforced *by* the legislature. If the lawmakers chose to ignore the rules, the courts would not intervene. The issue arose as early as the 1850s. The Supreme Court of Ohio thought it would be "most mischievous" to make the validity of every law depend upon the subjective judgment of judges around the state as to whether an act contained more than one subject or whether the title of the act clearly expressed the subject. A few years later, the Supreme Court of Minnesota rejected Ohio's position. The Minnesota court said that the constitution's procedural rules, which were meant to defeat a "vicious system" of "tricks and *finesse*," were senseless if they were merely directory.

The Minnesota court decided that the rule requiring bills to be read "at length" was mandatory, but some other courts disagreed. Legislators everywhere found the rule so impractical that they generally disregarded it. Most constitutions allowed them to dispense with the rule by a supermajority vote. Such votes became routine. Often, though, the lawmakers simply ignored the rule. Where they couldn't get away with that, they might have several legislative clerks read different bills simultaneously, a practice that literally complied with the constitution but was a pure waste of time.

Legislatures also found ways around the substantive restrictions imposed by the reform constitutions, sometimes with the connivance of courts and often with the support of the people. Indiana's experience with railroad aid is instructive. The constitutional convention had been dead set against state involvement with internal improvement schemes. It had also prohibited counties from lending their credit to any corporation and from borrowing money in order to purchase corporate stock. However, the constitution expressly allowed counties to buy corporate stock if they paid for it at the time of subscription, and it said nothing about cities and towns. When the Anderson *Courier* announced in 1869 that "no city, county or township were ever injured by having too many railroads," it reflected the same belief of every community in the 1830s that a local canal or railroad connection would bring on a golden age. In the 1860s the Indiana legislature passed general laws authorizing local governments to aid railroad construction via stock subscriptions or donations of money or bonds to railroad companies. Dozens of cities, counties, and townships provided aid with the approval of local voters. Even the severe depression of the 1870s only slowed but did not halt the flow of largesse. Between 1876 and 1886, forty-five townships and cities voted aid. The Indiana Supreme Court upheld stock subscriptions by counties in 1870. It never directly decided the question of donations, and so donations were made.

The saga of the Cincinnati Southern Railway is also revealing. Cincinnatians, seeing the diversion of their trade to Louisville and Nashville, wanted a railroad running south. A lawyer named Ferguson, reading the Ohio constitution literally, saw nothing in it to prohibit a city from building its own railroad, even one located primarily in another state. In 1869 the General Assembly authorized Cincinnati to issue bonds to the tune of $10 million for the construction of a city-owned railroad. When a taxpayer challenged the Ferguson Law, the Ohio Supreme Court conceded that the constitutional convention probably would have prohibited such statutes if it had foreseen them; but since the constitution did not expressly prohibit municipal ownership of internal improvements, the court upheld the law.

The nation's leading authority on railroad law criticized the Ohio court for exercising its "zeal and ingenuity" to sustain a law that deliberately evaded the plain intent of the constitutional convention to prohibit all modes of assisting railroad construction. By the late 1870s, Ohio judges were beginning to think that the case had been wrongly decided. Eventually, the city, which had leased the railroad to a private company on terms inadequate to service the bonds, decided that the whole enterprise had been a mistake. The schemes it devised to get out of the railroad business led to more lawsuits and more legal contortions by the court.

We are faced, then, with a strange situation in the late nineteenth century. The reputations of state legislatures remained as abysmal as ever, constitutional conventions continued to impose all kinds of procedural and substantive restraints on government, and the many sad experiences of government with economic development schemes seemed to justify both the reputation and the restraints. Yet voters continued to believe that government promotion of economic development would produce bonanzas.

There are various reasons for this anomaly. Memories are short and glittering visions powerful. Business interests, politicians, and communities, for reasons of their own, looked for ways to evade constitutional restrictions. The enormous size and influence of railroad and industrial corporations made even skeptics look to government as a counterbalance, and that opened the door to all kinds of governmental activity that in former times might not even have been thought of. It must be remembered, too, that government promotion of economic development had not been uniformly catastrophic. If it had been, perhaps lawmakers, judges, and citizens would have resisted the siren calls of promotionalism in the post-Civil War era. But the Erie Canal had been a glorious success. Ohio's state canals, built, like the Erie, before the Panic of 1837, had turned a profit. A history of Michigan credits the state-sponsored projects with spurring private railroad development by demonstrating the possibility of success and laying out the routes that private developers would follow. After the Civil War, government land grants to railroads practically built North Dakota. In short, there have always been enough positive results from public economic development efforts to keep the old promotional tradition alive. And so we have a continuous tug-of-war between those who want an activist government to promote development for the common good and those who fear government as tool of powerful men and organizations and a threat to individual liberty.

Historian Charles Postel sees something incongruous in the rise of the modern Tea Party. Seeing a causal connection between the federal government's "conservative market fundamentalist policies"—deregulation, reduced taxes on corporations and the wealthy, general expansion of the power of the market—before 2008 and the financial meltdown of that year, Postel thinks the Tea Party's hostility toward active government is irrational. But, he continues, the Tea Party's attitude can be understood as the rational, "hardheaded pursuit of self-interest" by older, white folks who sense the rise of other demographic groups with a stake in health care reforms and government services.

This is an analysis that no Tea Partier would accept. As Charles Pearson, a critic of Postel, observes, what Tea Party activists fear is "centralized, technocratic authority," the "fundamental transformation" of the country, and the "eclipsing of their own sovereignty as 'the people.'" Pearson describes the "Tea Party project" as one "steeped in constitutionalist politics" and aimed at reinvigorating "the power of the individual against the state." Like the mid-nineteenth century constitutional convention movement, today's Tea Party rests on the belief that government can't be trusted.

Many factors contributed to the constitutional convention movement of the 1840s. Not all of them had a Tea Party nature. Crowded court dockets, for example, were a common concern and arguably the single most important impetus behind the calling of conventions, at least in the existing states. In the territories, of course, it was the desire for statehood that produced the conventions. What gave the convention movement its Tea Party flavor was not a rational calculation of interest but a deeply felt distrust of government—a sense that government was incompetent, unfair, dishonest. Government may be necessary, the conventioneers thought, but it had to be restrained and accountable. Perhaps scholarly analysts would find other motivations or agendas concealed, consciously or unconsciously, behind the words in which advocates of the constitutional conventions called for reform, just as scholars and pundits today see anxieties or designs not announced in Tea Party programs. But regardless of whether the mid-nineteenth century arguments for constitutional conventions or the Tea Party program of today is taken at face value, there is an obvious kinship between the two movements that should enlighten and enliven the debate over the place of the modern Tea Party in American history.

Notes

1 Harry L. Watson, *Liberty and Power: The Politics of Jacksonian America*, 1st rev. ed. (New York: Hill & Wang, 2006), 237–43.

2 Michael Patrick Leahy, *Covenant of Liberty: The Ideological Origins of the Tea Party Movement* (New York: HarperCollins/Broadside, 2012), 230.

3 Millard H. Ruud, "No Law Shall Embrace More Than One Subject," *Minnesota Law Review* 42 (January 1958): 389–92.

4 Gordon S. Wood, *The Radicalism of the American Revolution* (New York: Knopf, 1992), 232–33.

5 Peter J. Galie and Christopher Bopst, *The New York State Constitution*, 2nd ed. (New York: Oxford University Press, 2012), 10–11, 14; Peter J. Galie, *Ordered Liberty: A Constitutional History of New York* (New York: Fordham University Press, 1996), 76–77.

6 Stuart Bruchey, *Enterprise: The Dynamic Economy of a Free People* (Cambridge, MA: Harvard University Press, 1990), 206.

7 Edmund Thornton Miller, *A Financial History of Texas* (Austin: University of Texas, 1916), 26.

8 James A. Henretta, "The Strange Birth of Liberal America: Michael Hoffman and the New York Constitution of 1846," *New York History* 77 (April 1996): 169.

9 Logan Esarey, *Internal Improvements in Early Indiana* (Indianapolis: Edward J. Hecker, 1912), 51, 80.

10 Alice E. Smith, *From Exploration to Statehood*, vol. 1 of *The History of Wisconsin*, ed. William Fletcher Thompson (Madison: State Historical Society of Wisconsin, 1973), 436.

11 Smith, *Exploration to Statehood*, 665.

[12] Alexander Davidson and Bernard Stuvé, *A Complete History of Illinois from 1673 to 1884* (Springfield: H. W. Rokker, 1884), 433.

[13] Theodore Calvin Pease, *The Frontier State, 1818–1848*, vol. 2 of *The Sesquicentennial History of Illinois* (1918; Urbana: University of Illinois Press, 1987), 52.

[14] Pease, *Frontier State*, 193.

[15] Pease, *Frontier State*, 211.

[16] *Journal of the House of Representatives of the Tenth General Assembly of the State of Illinois* (Vandalia: William Walters, 1836 [sic]), 680–83 (2 February 1837).

[17] Pease, *Frontier State*, 216.

[18] *Sangamo Journal*, 26 December 1844.

[19] Arthur Charles Cole, ed., *The Constitutional Debates of 1847*, vol. 14 of the Collections of the Illinois State Historical Library, Constitutional Series vol. 2 (Springfield: Trustees of the Illinois State Historical Library, 1919), xxii, xxix.

[20] *Chicago Democrat*, 24 August 1847, quoted in Cole, *Constitutional Debates*, xxix.

[21] Willis F. Dunbar and George S. May, *Michigan: A History of the Wolverine State* (Grand Rapids: Eerdmans, 1980), 366.

[22] Hugh Mculloch, *Men and Measures of Half a Century* (New York: Scribner's, 1889), 215–16.

[23] Justin E. Walsh, *Centennial History of the Indiana General Assembly, 1816–1978* (Indianapolis: Select Committee on the Centennial History of the Indiana General Assembly, 1987), 32.

[24] William Elsey Connelley and E. M. Coulter, *History of Kentucky*, 5 vols. (Chicago: American Historical Society, 1922), 2:724.

[25] Richard L. Morton, "The Virginia State Debt and Internal Improvements, 1820–38" *Journal of Political Economy* 25 (April 1917): 347.

[26] Morton, "Virginia State Debt," 367.

[27] Robert P. Sutton, *Revolution to Secession: Constitution Making in the Old Dominion* (Charlottesville: University Press of Virginia, 1989), 129–30.

[28] A. E. Dick Howard, *Commentaries on the Constitution of Virginia*, 2 vols. (Charlottesville: University Press of Virginia, 1974), 2:1,024.

[29] William Anderson, *A History of the Constitution of Minnesota, with the First Verified Text* (Minneapolis: University of Minnesota, 1921), 185.

Bibliographical Note

Primary sources

Most of the eighteenth- and nineteenth-century sources quoted in the book can be found online. Almost all of the state constitutions discussed are reprinted in *Sources and Documents of United States Constitutions*, edited by William F. Swindler, 12 vols. (Dobbs Ferry, NY: Oceana, 1973–88). They can also be found at various websites. Many of the reports of the convention proceedings are also available online. Bibliographical information for the published debates of the mid-nineteenth-century constitutional conventions in each of the states of the Old Northwest, as well as Minnesota, Kentucky, and Virginia, is listed below, together with links to sites where the text of each constitution, old and new, can be found and links to electronic versions of the debates. An asterisk indicates that a source can be readily accessed via Google Books (http://books.google.com/advanced_book_search). Some convention proceedings are available through the Hathi Trust, Internet Archive, and Making of America digital libraries.

Illinois

Constitutions: Emil Joseph Verlie, ed., *Illinois Constitutions*, Collections of the Illinois State Historical Library, vol. 13, Constitutional Series, vol. 1 (Springfield: Trustees of the Illinois State Historical Library, 1919) (https://archive.org/stream/collections ofill13illi#page/n13/mode/2up).

Convention proceedings: Arthur Charles Cole, ed., *The Constitutional Debates of 1847*, Collections of the Illinois State Historical Library, vol. 14, Constitutional Series, vol. 2 (Springfield: Trustees of the Illinois State Historical Library, 1919) (https://archive.org/details/constitutionaldeooilli).

See also http://wiu.libguides.com/content.php?pid=365002& sid=3004722, which has links to both the constitutions and the convention debates.

Indiana

Constitutions: *Charles Kettleborough, *Constitution Making in Indiana: A Source Book of Constitutional Documents with Historical Introduction and Critical Notes*, vol. 1: 1759–1851 (Indianapolis: Indiana Historical Commission, 1916). This volume includes the constitutions of 1816 and 1851 and many other documents.

Convention proceedings: H. Fowler, *Report of the Debates and Proceedings of the Convention for the Revision of the Constitution of the State of Indiana*, 2 vols. (Indianapolis: A. H. Brown, 1850–51). Both volumes are in the Making of America digital library. Volume 1 is published at http://quod.lib.umich.edu/m/moa/ aew7738.0001.001/3?q1=report+of+the+debates+and+proceedin gs&view=image&size=100. Volume 2 is available at Google Books.

Kentucky

Constitutions: *Bennett H. Young, *History and Texts of the Three Constitutions of Kentucky* (Louisville: Courier-Journal, 1890).

Convention proceedings: *R. Sutton, *Report of the Debates and Proceedings of the Convention for the Revision of the Constitution of the State of Kentucky* (Frankfort: A. G. Hodges, 1849).

Michigan

Constitutions: *Floyd Benjamin Streeter, *Political Parties in Michigan, 1837–1860: An Historical Study of Political Issues and Parties in Michigan from the Admission of the State to the Civil War* (Lansing: Michigan Historical Commission, 1918).

Convention proceedings: *Report of the Proceedings and Debates in the Convention to Revise the Constitution of the State of Michigan* (Lansing: R. W. Ingals, 1850).

Minnesota

Constitution: http://www.mnhs.org/library/constitution/.
Convention proceedings: Francis H. Smith, *The Debates and Proceedings of the Minnesota Constitutional Convention, including the Organic Act of the Territory* (St. Paul: Earle S. Goodrich, 1857) (http://quod.lib.umich.edu/cgi/t/text/text-idx?c=moa;idno =AHM5290).

Ohio

Constitutions:
http://ww2.ohiohistory.org/resource/database/funddocs.html.
Convention proceedings: *J. V. Smith, rptr., *Report of the Debates and Proceedings of the Convention for the Revision of the Constitution of the State of Ohio*, 2 vols. (Columbus: S. Medary, 1851).
For links to both the constitutions and the convention debates, see http://guides.law.csuohio.edu/ohioconstitutionprimarysources.

Virginia

Constitutions: http://vagovernmentmatters.org/primary-sourc es/browse/?tags=Foundations.
Convention proceedings: William G. Bishop, *Register of the Debates and Proceedings of the Va. Reform Convention* (Richmond: R. H. Gallaher, 1851).

Wisconsin

Constitutions:
https://www.wisconsinhistory.org/turningpoints/tp-015/.
Convention proceedings: *Milo M. Quaife, ed., *The Convention of 1846*, Collections of the State Historical Society of Wisconsin, vol. 27, Constitutional Series, vol. 2 (Madison: State Historical Society of Wisconsin, 1919); *H. A. Tenney et al., *Journal of the Convention to Form a Constitution for the State of Wisconsin, with a Sketch of the Debates, Begun and Held at Madison, on the Fifteenth Day of December, Eighteen Hundred and Forty-seven* (Madison, W. T.: Tenney, Smith & Holt, 1848). See also the following volumes edited by Milo M. Quaife: *The Movement for*

Statehood, 1845–1846, Collections of the State Historical Society of Wisconsin, vol. 26, Constitutional Series, vol. 1 (Madison: State Historical Society of Wisconsin, 1918); **The Struggle Over Ratification, 1846–1847*, Collections of the State Historical Society of Wisconsin, vol. 28, Constitutional Series, vol. 3 (Madison: State Historical Society of Wisconsin, 1920); *The Attainment of Statehood*, Collections of the State Historical Society of Wisconsin, vol. 29, Constitutional Series, vol. 4 (Madison: State Historical Society of Wisconsin, 1928).

Secondary Sources

The modern works on the Tea Party referred to in the Introduction and the Epilogue are Dick Armey and Matt Kibbe, *Give Us Liberty: A Tea Party Manifesto* (New York: William Morrow, 2010); Elizabeth Price Foley, *The Tea Party: Three Principles* (New York: Cambridge University Press, 2012); Ronald P. Formisano, *The Tea Party: A Brief History* (Johns Hopkins University Press, 2012); Michael Patrick Leahy, *Covenant of Liberty: The Ideological Origins of the Tea Party Movement* (New York: HarperCollins/Broadside, 2012); Jill Lepore, *The Whites of Their Eyes: The Tea Party's Revolution and the Battle over American History* (Princeton, NJ: Princeton University Press, 2010); Charles Pearson, "The Professors and the Tea Parties," http://reason.com/archives/2012/10/23/the-professors-and-the-tea-parties, 23 October 2012; Charles Postel, "The Tea Party in Historical Perspective: A Conservative Response to a Crisis of Political Economy," in *Steep: The Precipitous Rise of the Tea Party*, edited by Lawrence Rosenthal and Christine Trost (Berkeley: University of California Press, 2012); Scott Rasmussen and Doug Shoen, *Mad as Hell: How the Tea Party Movement is Fundamentally Remaking Our Two-Party System* (New York: HarperCollins, 2010); and Elliot A. Rosen, *The Republican Party in the Age of Roosevelt: Sources of Anti-Government Conservatism in the United States* (Charlottesville: University of Virginia Press, 2014).

Much of the information in Chapters 2, 3, and 8 on the Northwest Territory, the mill acts, Ohio history, and laissez-faire constitutionalism comes from my own research. Publications include "Public Aid to Private Enterprise Under the Ohio Constitution: Sections 4, 6, and 13, of Article VIII in Historical Perspective," *University of Toledo Law Review* 16 (Winter 1985): 405–64; *Democracy in Session: A History of the Ohio General Assembly* (Athens: Ohio University Press, 2009); "Eminent Domain and Economic Development: The Mill Acts and the Origins of Laissez-Faire Constitutionalism," *Journal of Libertarian Studies* 21 (Summer 2007): 101–22; and "Democrats, Whigs, and the Antebellum Origins of Laissez-Faire Constitutionalism," *New England Journal of History*, 57 (2000): 43–57.

Each book in the Oxford Commentaries on the State Constitutions of the U.S. series, originally published by Greenwood Press or Praeger, includes a historical background to the constitution analyzed in the book. The volumes all bear the same title, except for the name of the state (for example, *The Indiana State Constitution*). Many are now in a second edition. For a few states, none of them in the Old Northwest, there has yet to be a first edition.

For the background to each state's constitutional convention, particularly with regard to internal improvements and banking, I relied on one or two secondary sources per state. These sources are not cited in the notes, except to document direct quotations. Nor do the notes include other sources to which I resorted occasionally, again except to document a quotation. For Ohio, my major secondary source is my own *Democracy in Session*, cited above. For the other states, they are Theodore Calvin Pease, *The Frontier State, 1818–1848*, vol. 2 of *The Sesquicentennial History of Illinois* (1918; Urbana: University of Illinois Press, 1987); Logan Esarey, *A History of Indiana from Its Exploration to 1850*, 2nd ed., vol. 1 (Indianapolis: B. F. Bowen, 1918); Justin E. Walsh, *Centennial History of the Indiana General Assembly, 1816–1978* (Indianapolis: Select Committee on the Centennial History of the Indiana General Assembly, 1987); Willis F. Dunbar and George S. May, *Michigan: A History of the Wolverine State* (Grand Rapids: Eerdmans, 1980); Alice E. Smith, *From Exploration to Statehood*, vol. 1 of *The History of Wisconsin*, ed. William Fletcher Thompson (Madison: State Historical Society of Wisconsin, 1973).

Visit us at *www.quidprobooks.com*.

Made in the USA
Charleston, SC
10 March 2016